Postcolonialism: A Very Short Introduction

VERY SHORT INTRODUCTIONS are for anyone wanting a stimulating and accessible way in to a new subject. They are written by experts, and have been published in more than 25 languages worldwide.

The series began in 1995, and now represents a wide variety of topics in history, philosophy, religion, science, and the humanities. Over the next few years it will grow to a library of around 200 volumes – a Very Short Introduction to everything from ancient Egypt and Indian philosophy to conceptual art and cosmology.

Very Short Introductions available now:

ANCIENT PHILOSOPHY
Julia Annas
THE ANGLO-SAXON AGE
John Blair
ANIMAL RIGHTS
David DeGrazia
ARCHAEOLOGY   Paul Bahn
ARCHITECTURE
Andrew Ballantyne
ARISTOTLE   Jonathan Barnes
ART THEORY   Cynthia Freeland
THE HISTORY OF
ASTRONOMY   Michael Hoskin
ATHEISM   Julian Baggini
AUGUSTINE   Henry Chadwick
BARTHES   Jonathan Culler
THE BIBLE   John Riches
BRITISH POLITICS
Anthony Wright
BUDDHA   Michael Carrithers
BUDDHISM   Damien Keown
THE CELTS   Barry Cunliffe
CHOICE THEORY
Michael Allingham
CLASSICS   Mary Beard and
John Henderson
CLAUSEWITZ   Michael Howard
THE COLD WAR
Robert McMahon
CONTINENTAL PHILOSOPHY
Simon Critchley

COSMOLOGY   Peter Coles
CRYPTOGRAPHY
Fred Piper and Sean Murphy
DARWIN   Jonathan Howard
DEMOCRACY   Bernard Crick
DESCARTES   Tom Sorell
DRUGS   Leslie Iversen
THE EARTH   Martin Redfern
EIGHTEENTH-CENTURY
BRITAIN   Paul Langford
EMOTION   Dylan Evans
EMPIRE   Stephen Howe
ENGELS   Terrell Carver
ETHICS   Simon Blackburn
THE EUROPEAN UNION
John Pinder
EVOLUTION
Brian and Deborah Charlesworth
FASCISM   Kevin Passmore
THE FRENCH REVOLUTION
William Doyle
FREUD   Anthony Storr
GALILEO   Stillman Drake
GANDHI   Bhikhu Parekh
GLOBALIZATION
Manfred Steger
HEGEL   Peter Singer
HEIDEGGER   Michael Inwood
HINDUISM   Kim Knott
HISTORY   John H. Arnold
HOBBES   Richard Tuck

Available soon:

For more information visit our web site
www.oup.co.uk/vsi

Robert J. C. Young

POST-
COLONIALISM

A Very Short Introduction

OXFORD
UNIVERSITY PRESS

OXFORD
UNIVERSITY PRESS

Great Clarendon Street, Oxford OX2 6DP

Oxford University Press is a department of the University of Oxford.
It furthers the University's objective of excellence in research, scholarship,
and education by publishing worldwide in

Oxford New York

Auckland Bangkok Buenos Aires Cape Town Chennai
Dar es Salaam Delhi Hong Kong Istanbul Karachi Kolkata
Kuala Lumpur Madrid Melbourne Mexico City Mumbai Nairobi
São Paulo Shanghai Taipei Tokyo Toronto

Oxford is a registered trade mark of Oxford University Press
in the UK and in certain other countries

Published in the United States
by Oxford University Press Inc., New York

© Robert J. C. Young 2003

British Library Cataloguing in Publication Data

Data available

Library of Congress Cataloging in Publication Data

Data available

ISBN 0–19–280182–1

1 3 5 7 9 10 8 6 4 2

Typeset by RefineCatch Ltd, Bungay, Suffolk
Printed in Spain by Book Print S. L., Barcelona

For Yasmine

Contents

Acknowledgements

Many people have helped me with the writing of this book. Some sections from it have been given as papers in various parts of the world, and each audience's response has guided me in invaluable ways. For detailed discussion of individual topics, I would particularly like to thank Sadiq Ahmad, Jeeva and Prathima Anandan, Tanya Datta, Indira Ghose, Lucy Graham, Azzedine Haddour, Diana Hinds, Neil Lazarus, Roger Little, Paul Mylrea, Bernard O'Donoghue, Benita Parry, Ato Quayson, Rob Raeside, Neelam Srivastava, Weimin Tang, Skip Thompson, Megan Vaughan, and Else Vieira. I am also very grateful to the following people who have given me extensive help, often at short notice: Bashir Abu-Manneh offered me the benefit of his knowledge of Middle-Eastern politics and culture, and diligently corrected my Arabic. Elleke Boehmer read the manuscript and talked through many of the issues with me in a productive and positive way. Zia Ghaussy and Matthew Meadows gave me good advice on the journey from Kabul to Jalozai. Sahar Sobhi Abdel Hakim generously helped me over a number of detailed issues relating to women in Egypt and the Middle East more generally. Rita Kothari taught me how to think about translations beyond my own languages. Parvati Nair first introduced me to raï as well as to the issues discussed here with respect to Spanish-Moroccan immigration, and offered constructive responses to much of the material in the book. Rajeswari Sunder Rajan has always kept a severe eye on my writings, with friendship, charm, and humour. Joy Wang read several of the sections and gave me sound advice on the limits of the possible. Homi Bhabha has provided warm counsel throughout on many matters relating (and not relating) to the material here. I would also like to thank Badral Kaler for her generous support and forbearance, and Maryam, Yasmine, and Isaac for just being themselves.

List of illustrations

The publisher and the author apologize for any errors or omissions in the above list. If contacted they will be pleased to rectify these at the earliest opportunity.

Introduction
Montage

Have you ever been the only person of your own colour or ethnicity in a large group or gathering? It has been said that there are two kinds of white people: those who have never found themselves in a situation where the majority of people around them are not white, and those who have been the only white person in the room. At that moment, for the first time perhaps, they discover what it is really like for the other people in their society, and, metaphorically, for the rest of the world outside the west: to be from a minority, to live as the person who is always in the margins, to be the person who never qualifies as the norm, the person who is not authorized to speak.

This is as true for peoples as for persons. Do you feel that your own people and country are somehow always positioned outside the mainstream? Have you ever felt that the moment you said the word 'I', that 'I' was someone else, not you? That in some obscure way, you were not the subject of your own sentence? Do you ever feel that whenever you speak, you have already in some sense been spoken for? Or that when you hear others speaking, that you are only ever going to be the object of their speech? Do you sense that those speaking would never think of trying to find out how things seem to you, from where you are? That you live in a world of others, a world that exists *for* others?

How can we find a way to talk about this? That is the first question which postcolonialism tries to answer. Since the early 1980s, postcolonialism has developed a body of writing that attempts to shift the dominant ways in which the relations between western and non-western people and their worlds are viewed. What does that mean? It means turning the world upside down. It means looking from the other side of the photograph, experiencing how differently things look when you live in Baghdad or Benin rather than Berlin or Boston, and understanding why. It means realizing that when western people look at the non-western world what they see is often more a mirror image of themselves and their own assumptions than the reality of what is really there, or of how people outside the west actually feel and perceive themselves. If you are someone who does not identify yourself as western, or as somehow not completely western even though you live in a western country, or someone who is part of a culture and yet excluded by its dominant voices, inside yet outside, then postcolonialism offers you a way of seeing things differently, a language and a politics in which your interests come first, not last.

Postcolonialism claims the right of all people on this earth to the same material and cultural well-being. The reality, though, is that the world today is a world of inequality, and much of the difference falls across the broad division between people of the west and those of the non-west. This division between the rest and the west was made fairly absolute in the 19th century by the expansion of the European empires, as a result of which nine-tenths of the entire land surface of the globe was controlled by European, or European-derived, powers. Colonial and imperial rule was legitimized by anthropological theories which increasingly portrayed the peoples of the colonized world as inferior, childlike, or feminine, incapable of looking after themselves (despite having done so perfectly well for millennia) and requiring the paternal rule of the west for their own best interests (today they are deemed to require 'development'). The basis of such anthropological theories was the concept of race. In simple terms, the west–non-west relation was thought of in terms of whites versus the non-white races. White

2

culture was regarded (and remains) the basis for ideas of legitimate government, law, economics, science, language, music, art, literature – in a word, civilization.

Throughout the period of colonial rule, colonized people contested this domination through many forms of active and passive resistance. It was only towards the end of the 19th century, however, that such resistance developed into coherent political movements: for the peoples of most of the earth, much of the 20th century involved the long struggle and eventual triumph against colonial rule, often at enormous cost of life and resources. In Asia, in Africa, in Latin America, people struggled against the politicians and administrators of European powers that ruled empires or the colonists who had settled their world.

When national sovereignty had finally been achieved, each state moved from colonial to autonomous, postcolonial status. Independence! However, in many ways this represented only a beginning, a relatively minor move from direct to indirect rule, a shift from colonial rule and domination to a position not so much of independence as of being in-dependence. It is striking that despite decolonization, the major world powers did not change substantially during the course of the 20th century. For the most part, the same (ex-)imperial countries continue to dominate those countries that they formerly ruled as colonies. The cases of Afghanistan, Cuba, Iran, and Iraq, make it clear that any country that has the nerve to resist its former imperial masters does so at its peril. All governments of these countries that have positioned themselves politically against western control have suffered military interventions by the west against them.

Yet the story is not wholly negative. The winning of independence from colonial rule remains an extraordinary achievement. And if power remains limited, the balance of power is slowly changing. For one thing, along with this shift from formal to informal empire, the western countries require ever more additional labour power at home, which they fulfil through immigration. As a result of immigration, the clear division between the west and the rest in ethnic terms at least no longer operates absolutely. This is not to say that the president of the United States has ever been an African-American woman, or that Britain has elected an Asian Muslim as prime minister. Power remains carefully controlled. How many faces of power can you think of that are brown? The ones, that is, that appear on the front pages of the newspapers, where the everyday politics of world power are reported. Cultures are changing though: white Protestant America is being hispanized. Hispanic and black America have become the dynamic motors of much live western culture that operates beyond the graveyard culture of the heritage industry. Today, for many of the youth of Europe, Cuban culture rules, energizing and electrifying with its vibrant *son* and *salsa*. More generally, in terms of broad consensus, the dominance of western culture, on which much of the division between western and non-western peoples was assumed to rest in colonial times, has been dissolved into a more generous system of cultural respect and a tolerance for differences. Some of the limits of that respect will be explored in later sections of this book.

For now, what is important is that postcolonialism involves first of all the argument that the nations of the three non-western continents (Africa, Asia, Latin America) are largely in a situation of subordination to Europe and North America, and in a position of economic inequality. Postcolonialism names a politics and philosophy of activism that contests that disparity, and so continues in a new way the anti-colonial struggles of the past. It asserts not just the right of African, Asian, and Latin American peoples to access resources and material well-being, but also the dynamic power of their cultures, cultures that are now intervening in and transforming the societies of the west.

Postcolonial cultural analysis has been concerned with the elaboration of theoretical structures that contest the previous dominant western ways of seeing things. A simple analogy would be

4

with feminism, which has involved a comparable kind of project: there was a time when any book you might read, any speech you might hear, any film that you saw, was always told from the point of view of the male. The woman was there, but she was always an object, never a subject. From what you would read, or the films you would see, the woman was always the one who was looked at. She was never the observing eye. For centuries it was assumed that women were less intelligent than men and that they did not merit the same degree of education. They were not allowed a vote in the political system. By the same token, any kind of knowledge developed by women was regarded as non-serious, trivial, gossip, or alternatively as knowledge that had been discredited by science, such as superstition or traditional practices of childbirth or healing. All these attitudes were part of a larger system in which women were dominated, exploited, and physically abused by men. Slowly, but increasingly, from the end of the 18th century, feminists began to contest this situation. The more they contested it, the more it became increasingly obvious that these attitudes extended into the whole of the culture: social relations, politics, law, medicine, the arts, popular and academic knowledges.

As a politics and a practice, feminism has not involved a single system of thought, inspired by a single founder, as was the case with Marxism or psychoanalysis. It has rather been a collective work, developed by different women in different directions: its projects have been directed at a whole range of phenomena of injustice, from domestic violence to law and language to philosophy. Feminists have also had to contend with the fact that relations between women themselves are not equal and can in certain respects duplicate the same kinds of power hierarchies that exist between women and men. Yet at the same time, broadly speaking feminism has been a collective movement in which women from many different walks of life have worked towards common goals, namely the emancipation and empowerment of women, the right to make decisions that affect their own lives, and the right to have equal access to the law, to education, to medicine, to the workplace, in the process changing those institutions themselves so that they no longer continue to represent only male interests and perspectives.

In a comparable way, 'postcolonial theory' involves a conceptual reorientation towards the perspectives of knowledges, as well as needs, developed outside the west. It is concerned with developing the driving ideas of a political practice morally committed to transforming the conditions of exploitation and poverty in which large sections of the world's population live out their daily lives. Some of this theoretical work has gained a reputation for obscurity and for involving complex ideas that ordinary people are not able to understand. When faced with the authority of theory produced by academics, people often assume that their own difficulties of comprehension arise from a deficiency in themselves. This is unfortunate, since many of these ideas were never produced by academics in the first place and can be understood relatively easily once the actual situations that they describe are understood. For this reason, this book seeks to introduce postcolonialism in a way not attempted before: rather than explaining it top down, that is elaborating the theory in abstract terms and then giving a few examples, it seeks to follow the larger politics of postcolonialism which are fundamentally populist and affirm the worth of ordinary people and their cultures. Postcolonialism will here be elaborated not from a top-down perspective but from below: the bulk of the sections that follow will start with a situation and then develop the ideas that emerge from its particular perspective. What you will get, therefore, is postcolonialism without the obscure theory, postcolonialism from below, which is what and where it should rightly be, given that it elaborates a politics of 'the subaltern', that is, subordinated classes and peoples.

Postcolonial theory, so-called, is not in fact a theory in the scientific sense, that is a coherently elaborated set of principles that can predict the outcome of a given set of phenomena. It comprises instead a related set of perspectives, which are juxtaposed against one another, on occasion contradictorily. It involves issues that are often the preoccupation of other disciplines and activities, particularly to do with the position of women, of development, of ecology, of social justice, of socialism in its broadest sense. Above all, postcolonialism seeks to intervene, to force its alternative knowledges into the power structures of the west as well as the non-west. It seeks to change the way people think, the way they behave, to produce a more just and equitable relation between the different peoples of the world.

For this reason, there will be no attempt here to elaborate postcolonialism as a single set of ideas, or as a single practice. At one level there is no single entity called 'postcolonial theory': postcolonialism, as a term, describes practices and ideas as various as those within feminism or socialism. The book therefore is not written as a series of chapters that develop an overall thesis or argument as in the standard model of academic writing. Instead it uses the technique of montage to juxtapose perspectives and times against one another, seeking to generate a creative set of relations between them. For much of postcolonial theory is not so much about static ideas or practices, as about the relations between ideas and practices: relations of harmony, relations of conflict, generative relations between different peoples and their cultures. Postcolonialism is about a changing world, a world that has been changed by struggle and which its practitioners intend to change further.

Montage

A lot of people don't like the term 'postcolonial': now you may begin to see why. It disturbs the order of the world. It threatens privilege and power. It refuses to acknowledge the superiority of western cultures. Its radical agenda is to demand equality and well-being for all human beings on this earth.

You will now be migrating through that postcolonial earth: the chapters that follow will take you on a journey through its cities, the suburbs of its dispossessed, the poverty of its rural landscape.

Though these scenes are acknowledged to exist, many of them are invisible, the lives and daily experiences of their inhabitants even more so. The chapters of this book comprise different 'scenes', snapshots taken in various locations around the world and juxtaposed against one another. This book therefore amounts to a kind of photograph album, but not one in which you are just gazing at the image, made static and unreal, turned into an object divorced from the whispers of actuality. These are stories from the other side of photographs. Testimonies from the people who are looking at you as you read. The montage has been left as a rough cut that deliberately juxtaposes incompatible splintered elements. A series of shorts that stage the contradictions of the history of the present, by catching its images fleetingly at a standstill. These fragmentary moments also trace a larger journey of translation, from the disempowered to the empowered.

When we begin to teach 'marginality', we start with the source books of the contemporary study of the cultural politics of colonialism and its aftermath: the great texts of the 'Arab World', most often Frantz Fanon, a Christian psychiatrist from Martinique ... It is also from this general context that we find the source book in our discipline: Edward Said's *Orientalism* ... Said's book was not a study of marginality, nor even of marginalization. It was the study of the construction of an object, for investigation and control. The study of colonial discourse, directly released by work such as Said's, has, however, blossomed into a garden where the marginal can speak and be spoken, even spoken for.

Gayatri Chakravorty Spivak, *Outside in the Teaching Machine* (1993)

Chapter 1
Subaltern knowledge

You find yourself a refugee

You wake one morning from troubled dreams to discover that your world has been transformed. Under cover of night, you have been transported elsewhere. As you open your eyes, the first thing you notice is the sound of the wind blowing across flat, empty land.

You are walking with your family towards a living cemetery on the borderlands between Afghanistan and Pakistan. Towards Peshawar, city of flowers, city of spies. A frontier town, the first stop for travellers from Kabul who have passed out through the carved city gate of Torkham, down the long narrow curves of grey rock of the Khyber Pass to the flat plain that lies beyond, to the Grand Trunk Road that runs, stretches, streams all the way to Kolkata.

In the Old City, among the many shops and stalls in the Khyber Bazaar around the Darwash mosque, you will find a narrow street where the houses climb into the sky with their ornamented balconies exploding out towards each other. This street is known as the Qissa Khawani Bazaar, the street of storytellers. Over the centuries, fabulous intricate tales have been elaborated there between men relaxing over bubbling amber *shishas*, trying to outdo the professional storytellers, or amongst those more quickly sipping sweet, syrupy tea in glasses at the chai stalls. The stories that are being traded there now are not for you.

You are far to the west, beyond the colonial cantonment, beyond the huge suburbs of temporary housing of those who have arrived long since, out into the flats that lie before the mountains. The rest of your family, two of your children, are missing. You are carrying with you a bag of clothes, a mat, for prayer and sleep, a large plastic container for water, and some aluminium pots. Some soldiers on the road stop you from walking further. The Jalozai refugee camp near Peshawar has been closed. Pashtuns who arrive now from Afghanistan are shepherded towards Chaman, not a refugee camp but a 'waiting area'. Here, once your eye moves above tent level, the earth is flat and featureless until it hits the dusky distant shapes of the Himalayan foothills on the horizon.

Since this is not an official refugee camp, there is no one here to register you or mark your arrival as you slowly make your way forwards. While your children sit exhausted and hungry on the

1. New Jalozai refugee camp, Peshawar, Pakistan, November 2001: an Uzbek family that recently arrived in New Jalozai from Northern Afghanistan is seen here in their new home.

bare, sandy brown earth, the skin on their blown bellies marked with the crimson stars of infection, you go in search of water and food, and with the hope of being issued with materials for housing – three sticks of wood and a large plastic sheet. This will be your tent, where you and your family will live – that is, those who manage to survive the lack of food, the dehydration, the dysentery, the cholera.

You may leave within months. Or, if you are unlucky – like the Somali refugees in Kenya, the Palestinian refugees in Gaza, Jordan, Lebanon, Syria, the West Bank, or the 'internally displaced persons' in Sri Lanka or the South Africa of the 1970s – you may find that you are to be there for a decade, or for several This may be the only home you, your children, and your grandchildren will ever have.

Refugee: you are unsettled, uprooted. You have been translated. Who translated you? Who broke your links with the land? You have been forcibly moved off, or you have fled war or famine. You are mobile, mobilized, stumbling along your line of flight. But nothing flows. In moving, your life has come to a halt. Your life has been fractured, your family fragmented. The lovely dull familiar stabilities of ordinary everyday life and local social existence that

> How rich our mutability, how easily we change (and are changed) from one thing to another, how unstable our place – and all because of the missing foundation of our existence, the lost ground of our origin, the broken link with our land and our past. There are no Palestinians. Who are the Palestinians? 'The inhabitants of Judea and Samaria.' Non-Jews. Terrorists. Troublemakers. DPs. Refugees. Names on a card. Numbers on a list. Praised in speeches – *el pueblo palestino, il popolo palestino, le peuple palestin* – but treated as interruptions, intermittent presences.
>
> Edward W. Said, *After the Last Sky* (1986)

2. New Jalozai refugee camp, Peshawar, Pakistan, November 2001: a young Afghan boy flies a kite.

you have known have passed. Compressed into a brief moment, you have experienced the violent disruptions of capitalism, the end of the comforts of the commonplace. You have become an emblem of everything that people are experiencing in cold modernity across different times. You encounter a new world, a new culture to which you have to adapt while trying to preserve your own recognizable forms of identity. Putting the two together is an experience of pain. Perhaps one day you, or your children, will see it as a form of liberation, but not now. Life has become too fragile, too uncertain. You can count on nothing. You have become an object in the eyes of the world. Who is interested in your experiences now, in what you think or feel? Politicians of the world rush to legislate to prevent you from entry into their countries. Asylum seeker: barred.

You are the intruder. You are untimely, you are out of place. A refugee tearing yourself from your own land, carrying your body, beliefs, your language and your desires, your habits and your affections, across to the strange subliminal spaces of unrecognizable worlds. Everything that happens in this raw, painful experience of

12

disruption, dislocation, and dis-remembering paradoxically fuels the cruel but creative crucible of the postcolonial.

Different kinds of knowledge

One thing that you would be unlikely to do in the Jalozai camp is to read this book, even if you were literate, and it had been translated into Pushto. You would talk a lot, speak to many people about day-to-day problems, sometimes relating longer and harder tales of suffering amid war and famine, trying to make sense of your experiences. If you met any of those from elsewhere working for your support, you would most likely speak to them of your needs – for medicine, for food, shelter. You would not articulate your experiences for the benefit of others you would never meet, you would not translate your life into a story or a representation for others. Yet you are the not-so-silent hero of this book: it is written for you. Even if you will never read these words, they are written for you.

Whether you could read this book or not brings out one of the major ways in which the world is divided, though the line can be cut in many places. Whether you have clean water or not, whether you have adequate food and health care or not, whether you can read or not, whether or not you have formal education. Everyone has informal education, and the boundary lines between the formal and the informal are more than fluid. The knowledge that you need is the knowledge you learn informally. From your own family and environment. The knowledge you learn formally is someone else's knowledge. Who authorized it? Whose knowledge is it? The knowledge that you learn at different schools will not be the same, and the frame of mind in which you learn will not be the same either: think of the differences for children between those who attend private schools in the west costing £15,000 a year, and those who began the school year in 2001 at the Al-Khader school near Bethlehem. The school buildings had been destroyed by Israeli military action and the children had to learn in a tent. Or think about the learning experiences of the Palestinian girl in Figure 3, who walks to school through the ruins of the Rafah refugee camp

3. A Palestinian school girl walks in the ruins of a refugee camp in Rafah in southern Gaza Strip, 15 April 2001. This happened a day after Israeli forces attacked the camp in the second incursion in less than a week into an area that Israel handed over to full Palestinian control under interim peace deals.

where she lives, where the day before three Israeli tanks and two bulldozers had reduced the buildings to rubble.

Not a lot has changed in Palestine in the 50 years since schools were first held in the open air at Khan Yunis refugee camp, Gaza Strip, or at the Jalazone refugee camp in the West Bank. If they are still alive, those boys are now old men, living in refugee camps that are themselves habitual targets for military strikes. How does it feel to have lived through such a life?

Thinking of these schools today while you read will help to develop the perspectives from which postcolonialism is generated. Think of Al-Khader, of Beit Jala, of Jalozai, of Jalazone, of Jenin, of Khan Yunis, of Rafah. How does the life that people live there compare to mine or yours? Imagine what it is like to grow up in a close, deprived community, and then see it literally bulldozed to the ground on the

4. The early UNRWA school, Jalazone refugee camp, West Bank, 1951.

orders of the state. Read Bloke Modisane's account of the destruction of Sophiatown, the vibrant centre of black cultural life in Johannesburg, by the South African apartheid government in 1958.

> **Something in me died, a piece of me died, with the dying of Sophiatown ... In the name of slum clearance they had brought the bulldozers and gored into her body, and for a brief moment, looking down Good Street, Sophiatown was like one of its own many victims; a man gored by the knives of Sophiatown, lying in the open gutters, a raisin in the smelling drains, dying of multiple stab wounds, gaping wells gushing forth blood; the look of shock and bewilderment, of horror and incredulity, on the face of the dying man.**
>
> **Bloke Modisane, *Blame Me on History* (1963)**

Modisane doesn't allow us, though, to make the mistake of assuming that such experiences, differences between the privileged and the wretched of the earth, only involve the questions of suffering and deprivation. There are other kinds of riches, other kinds of loss. Other kinds of ways of thinking about the world. Human, rather than material.

The third world goes tricontinental

See a picture of children who are assembling at a school, standing barefoot on the stones, and you know you are in 'the third world'. This third world is the postcolonial world. The term 'third world' was originally invented on the model of the Third Estate of the French Revolution. The world was divided according to the two major political systems, capitalism and socialism, and these were the first and second worlds. The third world was made up of what was left over: the 'non-aligned' nations, the new independent nations that had formerly made up the colonies of the imperial powers. At the Bandung Conference of 1955, 29 mostly newly independent African and Asian countries, including Egypt, Ghana, India, and Indonesia, initiated what became known as the non-aligned movement. They saw themselves as an independent power bloc, with a new 'third world' perspective on political, economic, and cultural global priorities. It was an event of enormous importance; it symbolized the common attempt of the people of colour in the world to throw off the yoke of the white western nations. Politically, there was to be a third way, neither that of the west nor that of the Soviet bloc. However, that third way was slow to be defined or developed. The term gradually became associated with the economic and political problems that such countries encountered, and consequently with poverty, famine, unrest: 'the Gap'.

In many ways, the Bandung Conference marks the origin of postcolonialism as a self-conscious political philosophy. A more militant version of third-world politics, as a global alliance resisting the continuing imperialism of the west, came 11 years later at the great Tricontinental Conference held in Havana in 1966. For the first time, this brought Latin America (including the Caribbean) together with Africa and Asia, the three continents of the South – hence the name 'tricontinental'. In many ways, tricontinental is a more appropriate term to use than 'postcolonial'. The Tricontinental Conference established a journal (called simply *Tricontinental*) which for the first time brought together the writings of 'postcolonial' theorists and activists (Amilcar Cabral, ✓ Frantz Fanon, Che Guevara, Ho Chi Minh, Jean-Paul Sartre), elaborated not as a single political and theoretical position but as a transnational body of work with a common aim of popular liberation. Many postcolonial theorists in the United States, however, remain unaware of this radical antecedent to their own work: because of the US blockade of Cuba, the journal was not allowed to be imported into the country.

As terms, both 'tricontinental' and 'third world' retain their power because they suggest an alternative culture, an alternative

> The colonialists usually say that it was they who brought us into history: today we show that this is not so. They made us leave history, our history, to follow them, right at the back, to follow the progress of their history.
>
> Amilcar Cabral, *Return to the Source* (1973)

'epistemology', or system of knowledge. Most of the writing that has dominated what the world calls knowledge has been produced by people living in western countries in the past three or more centuries, and it is this kind of knowledge that is elaborated within and sanctioned by the academy, the institutional knowledge corporation. The origins of much of this knowledge, particularly mathematical and scientific, came from the Arab world, which is why today even westerners write in Arabic whenever they write a number. Much emphasis in western schools is placed on the Latin and Greek inheritance of western civilization, but most westerners remain completely unaware of

> What is the role that we, the exploited people of the world, must play? . . .
>
> The contribution that falls to us, the exploited and backward of the world, is to eliminate the foundations sustaining imperialism: our oppressed nations, from which capital, raw materials and cheap labor (both workers and technicians) are extracted, and to which new capital (tools of domination), arms and all kinds of goods are exported, sinking us into absolute dependence. The fundamental element of that strategic objective, then, will be the real liberation of the peoples . . .
>
> Che Guevara, 'Message to the Tricontinental' (1967)

MESSAGE
TO THE
TRICONTINENTAL

**MAJOR
ERNESTO
CHE GUEVARA**

RADIO HABANA CUBA

5. Che Guevara, 'Message to the Tricontinental', 16 April 1967. Sent 'from somewhere in the world' to the Organization of Solidarity of the Peoples of Asia, Africa, and Latin America (OSPAAAL), Guevara's one public statement made in the interval between his disappearance from Cuba in the spring of 1965 and his murder in Bolivia on 9 October 1967 was published in the first issue of *Tricontinental* magazine.

the fact that they read and write Arabic every day. Imagine the headline: 'Al-gebra banned in US schools after Al-Qaeda link discovered.'

Postcolonialism begins from its own knowledges, many of them more recently elaborated during the long course of the anti-colonial movements, and starts from the premise that those in the west, both within and outside the academy, should take such other knowledges, other perspectives, as seriously as those of the west. Postcolonialism, or tricontinentalism, is a general name for these insurgent knowledges that come from the subaltern, the dispossessed, and seek to change the terms and values under which we all live. You can learn it anywhere if you want to. The only qualification you need to start is to make sure that you are looking at the world not from above, but from below.

Burning their books

In *The Big Sea* (1940), the African-American novelist Langston Hughes tells the story of his leaving New York on a ship for Africa. He climbs to the top of the deck and throws all the books he has brought with him for the voyage as far as he can out into the sea. As they spin into the ocean one by one, he senses the exhilaration of freedom: 'It was like throwing a million bricks out of my heart when I threw the books into the water'. He is leaving behind everything he has known and been taught, on his way to the world from which his ancestors came. All the hierarchical culture, in which the African-American is put firmly at the bottom, can be discarded in the return to a continent in which he will be amongst his own people, with their own way of doing things:

> My Africa, motherland of the Negro peoples! And me a Negro! Africa! The real thing, to be touched and seen, not merely read about in a book.

When Hughes gets to Africa at last, one thing hurts him a lot when he talks to the people.

> The Africans looked at me and would not believe I was a Negro.
> 'I am a Negro, too.'

> But they only laughed at me and shook their heads and said: 'You, white man! You, white man!'.

Frantz Fanon had the opposite experience. In Martinique, he had always been considered one of the fair-skinned. On arrival in Lyon in France, however, he found that people called out in the street when they saw him: 'Look! A negro!'. Fanon comments:

> I came into the world imbued with the will to find a meaning in things, my spirit filled with the desire to attain to the source of the world, and then I found that I was an object in the midst of other objects.

Fanon's first response is to experience the pain of, as he puts it, being 'sealed into that crushing objecthood'. Later he realizes that the problem goes even deeper. That being turned into an object, the object of a pointing finger and a deriding gaze, is only the exterior part. What also happens is that those in such situations come to internalize this view of themselves, to see themselves as different, 'other', lesser.

I also was tired of learning and reciting poems in praise of daffodils, and my relations with the few 'real' English boys and girls I had met were awkward. I had discovered that if I called myself English they would snub me haughtily: 'You're not English; you're a horrid colonial'.

Jean Rhys, 'The Day They Burned the Books' (1968)

In 'The Day They Burned the Books', the white Creole novelist Jean Rhys tells the story of Mr Sawyer, a white steamship agent on a Caribbean island, who is married to a woman of colour whom he periodically abuses in drunken moments. At the back of his house Mr Sawyer builds a small room, which he lines with English books that he has specially sent out to him. His sickly 'half-caste' son Eddie is the first to challenge the assumption of the narrator, a young girl, that everything from 'home', that is England, is naturally superior to anything on the island. At the same time, Eddie borrows books from the library, and when his father dies, he takes possession of it. After a few days, Eddie and the narrator walk into the library to find Mrs Sawyer, who has patiently remained married for so many years, erupting in a rage of hate, pulling the books from the shelves, separating them all into two piles. The ones to be sold, and the ones to be burned. When she pulls one particular book off the shelf, Eddie pleads with her not to burn it, telling her that he is reading it. Eventually he snatches it from her, shrieking 'Now I've got to hate you too'. The narrator grabs one for herself too, and the children run out into the garden and to the street, and then sit together for a while in the darkness. Eddie begins to cry. In a gesture of sympathy for Eddie's profound loneliness, the girl asks Eddie what his book is. It is Kipling's *Kim*. She has not been so lucky. She instinctively feels her prize to be a momentous thing, but when she looks to see what it is, she is very disappointed, 'because it was in French and seemed dull. *Fort Comme La Mort*, it was called . . .'.

Jean Rhys' story reads as an allegory not of colonialism as such, but of the gendered power relations of colonialism, where decades of patriarchal exploitation and aggressive racial-cultural hatred are answered by Mrs Sawyer's violent rejection of the culture on which such superiority is founded. Eddie's contradictory reaction, hating his father, hating 'home', England, but wanting his father's books, brings him into conflict with his mother, whom he loves but who in turn hates all his father's books. Eddie's marginal place is between conflicting, competing cultures: identifying with one emotionally, curious about the other intellectually.

Such ambivalent attitudes and multiple identities are defined by the ✓
Zimbabwean novelist Tsitsi Dangarembga as the native's 'nervous
condition', his or her existence strung out between the incompatible
layers of different cultures. When an original culture is
superimposed with a colonial or dominant culture through
education, it produces a nervous condition of ambivalence,
uncertainty, a blurring of cultural boundaries, inside and outside,
an otherness within. In *Nervous Conditions* (1988), Tambudzai,
the narrator who dreams of education, walks into the house of her
headmaster relative who has adopted white ways. She finds that
she does not know where to sit, she does not know how to read the
conventional signs of a room, she does not know which language
to use – English or Shona? The individuals in such a society
are subject to the painfulness of what Fanon recognizes as a
hybridized split existence, trying to live as two different,
incompatible people at once. The negotiation between different
identities, between the layers of different value systems (especially
in the case of women, for whom the options seem to be mutually
contradictory) is part of the process of becoming white, changing
your race and your class by assimilating the dominant culture.
Except that, though you may assimilate white values, you never
quite can become white enough.

Book burning can be a gesture of liberation, or of powerlessness to
make a statement by any other means. Usually, of course, it is
generally thought of as oppressive, destructive, fascistic, as indeed it
is when it consists of a nationalist attack on minority cultures.
When agents of the Sinhalese United National Party burned down
the Jaffna University Library in May 1981, for example: 'Thousands
of Tamil books, manuscripts and *ola*, dried palm leaf, documents
were burnt, including the only copy of *Yalpanam Vaipavama*, a
history of Jaffna'. When in May 1992, Serb nationalist forces threw
incendiary grenades into the Oriental Institute (Orijentalni
institut) in Sarajevo, home to one of Europe's most important
collections of Islamic manuscripts: 'Virtually all of its contents were
consumed by the flames. Losses included 5,263 bound manuscripts

in Arabic, Persian, Turkish, Hebrew and local *alhamijado* – or *adzamijski* – (Serbo-Croat-Bosnian in Arabic script), as well as tens of thousands of Ottoman-era documents'. Ethnic cleansing involves destroying knowledge and histories as well as people.

'Bradford Muslims' has become a generic description not of Muslims who happen to live in Bradford, England, but of what are considered 'fundamentalist' Muslims in the west. On 14 January 1989 a group of Muslims in Bradford and Oldham publicly burned copies of Salman Rushdie's *The Satanic Verses*. Commentators rushed to compare them to the Nazi book-burners in Germany in 1933. By comparison, we may note that the burning of J. K. Rowling's *Harry Potter* books in the United States by fundamentalist Christian groups has received rather less press attention.

Rushdie's position was complex because up to that point he had been one of the most noticeable proponents of anti-racism in Britain, voicing the politics and perspectives of the migrant community. Suddenly it became clear that within the communities of the ethnic minorities for whom he spoke, there were very different attitudes from Rushdie's perspective of multicultural mixture (he calls it 'chutnification'), endorsed by other ethnic minority writers, such as Hanif Kureishi, and also by the media. There is a deep split between celebratory multiculturalism and the real situation of many minorities who experience oppression in their everyday lives.

For the west, this appears largely as a division between liberals and conservatives: the first accept assimilation, while the second want to retain their unsullied cultural identity. For minorities in the west, or for those living outside the west, the divisions are less clear-cut. It is not unusual for individuals to want both at the same time. The nervous condition of postcolonial desire finds itself haunted by an ungovernable ambivalence.

> The conflict of cultures and community around *The Satanic Verses* has been mainly represented in spatial terms and binary geopolitical polarities – Islamic fundamentalists vs. Western literary modernists, the quarrel of the ancient (ascriptive) migrants and modern (ironic) metropolitans. This obscures the anxiety of the irresolvable, borderline culture of hybridity that articulates its problems of identification and its diasporic aesthetic in an uncanny, disjunctive temporality that is, at once, the *time* of cultural displacement, and the *space* of the 'untranslatable'.
>
> Homi K. Bhabha, *The Location of Culture* (1994)

Chapter 2
History and power, from below and above

African and Caribbean revolutionaries in Harlem, 1924

I am looking at a photograph. Three men are standing together, posing quite stiffly and staring seriously and thoughtfully into the camera. Each is wearing a stylish suit, with a waistcoat and fob watch. The man in a white suit and wing tips in the centre wears a hat, the other two are carrying them. The shorter, slightly portly man on the right leans on the back of a folding wooden chair. Though they are posing together, the men keep physically separate from each other, suggesting that they are acquaintances but not close friends. There is an odd disjunction between the opulence of their outfits, and the rather run-down brick building behind them. It looks as though they are outside the back of an old tenement house or office building. The window behind has one shutter hanging to its right, but there is no corresponding shutter on the other side.

The photograph, taken by the famous photographer of the Harlem Renaissance James Van Der Zee, is of Marcus Garvey with George O. Marke and Prince Kojo Tovalou-Houénou, taken in August 1924. Garvey was from Jamaica, Marke from Sierre Leone, Tovalou-Houénou from Dahomey: they came together this day in New York City and are probably posing at the back of the former

6. Marcus Garvey with George O. Marke and Prince Kojo Tovalou-Houénou.

Black Star line offices at 56 West 135th Street in Harlem. Marke was supreme deputy potentate of the United Negro Improvement Association (UNIA): educated in Freetown and at the universities of Aberdeen and Edinburgh, Scotland, he had come to New York as a Sierre Leonean delegate to the 1920 UNIA convention. In 1922, he was appointed minister plenipotentiary to the UNIA delegation to the League of Nations, which petitioned the League to turn the former German colonies in Africa over to black settlement under the direction of the UNIA. The request was refused. The colonies were mandated to Britain and South Africa instead.

Garvey, founder of the UNIA, had by 1924 already been convicted on mail fraud charges by an FBI eager for an excuse to deport him. Having early joined Jamaica's 'National Club', which sought independence from Britain, Garvey had travelled widely in Central America and then gone to London, where his sister Adriana was a governess. In London, he learned of the Pan-African movement, which had held its first conference there in 1900, and read Booker T. Washington's *Up From Slavery*. Most significantly, he met and became friends with the great Sudanese-Egyptian nationalist Duse Mohammed Ali, and worked with him on his radical nationalist newspaper, the *African Times and Orient Review*. When he returned to Jamaica to found the Universal Negro Improvement Association in 1914, Garvey's political philosophy, based on a simple, powerful message of black power and pride, was already formed. Two years later, he was invited to the United States by Booker T. Washington himself. Probably no black immigrant to the United States has ever had more political impact. He translated anti-colonial rhetoric into the language of civil rights and black empowerment, and throughout the 20th century the two would move forward, inalienably bound together, propelling each other. This photograph records one such vector, one such enabling moment.

Prince Tovalou-Houénou, for his part, had just arrived in New York from France to speak at the 1924 UNIA Convention at Harlem's Liberty Hall. Tovalou-Houénou was president of the *Ligue Universelle de Défense de la Race Noire* (LDRN, the Universal League for the Defence of the Black Race), which he had founded in Paris after a famous incident in which some visiting white Americans had tried to have him thrown out of a café in Paris, on account of his being black. Looking at this aristocratic man, the nephew of the exiled King of Dahomey, it is easy to see why he resented such treatment so forcefully that he aroused the sympathy of the entire French press, as a result of which Paris for many years had the reputation of being the western city most sympathetic to black artists and intellectuals. Josephine Baker, Langston Hughes, James Baldwin, Chester Himes, Sidney Bechet: the French loved them – just as long as they weren't Arabs.

At that 1924 Convention, Garvey was able to announce that there were now some 14,000 branches of the UNIA movement. Half of them were in North America, the rest spread throughout the Caribbean, Central and South America, and Africa; total membership was estimated at 6 million. That extraordinary globalized constituency was mirrored in the title of Tovalou-Houénou's newspaper, *Les Continents*. Revolutionary movements across the Black Atlantic; three revolutionaries coming together in the United States from French and British colonies in Africa and the Caribbean in order to establish intercultural networks of activism and transnational solidarity.

Garvey's movements around the Caribbean, the United States, and England, make him an early example of what Salman Rushdie characterizes as the state of being a 'translated man', that is, someone who is 'translated' across cultures. This is not something that people necessarily experience in a passive way: Garvey's call for the restitution of the dignity of the black man was a call to self-translation. Translation is a way of thinking about how languages, people, and cultures are transformed as they move between different places. It can also be used more metaphorically, as a way of describing how the individual or the group can be transformed by changing their sense of their own place in society.

Here, standing in New York with each other, ready to speak to the assembled audience of the UNIA at Liberty Hall, were three men who had not simply made the journey to Harlem from Jamaica, Dahomey, and Sierre Leone. They were themselves active cultural translators in the process of refiguring American culture too, and beyond that cultures right across the globe. Their meeting marks a moment of the translation of revolutionary ideologies between nations of the oppressed. Tovalou-Houénou was subsequently persecuted by the French colonial authorities, and Garvey was required by the FBI to leave the United States. For decades afterwards, the links between American civil rights activists, such as the singer Paul Robeson, and Caribbean and African anti-colonial leaders, would be the subject of surveillance by the FBI, MI5, and MI6. But it was too late – Garvey's intervention had already been made. Caribbean radicalism had come to New York and London, and the cause of black empowerment would grow ever stronger. Generations of Caribbean radicals would follow in their footsteps to African-America: C. L. R. James, Claude McKay, George Padmore.

The most celebrated moment in this long history came in 1960 when Fidel Castro, having been mistreated in his midtown hotel,

7. Fidel Castro returns to Harlem, 1995.

Castro revisits Harlem

On his visit to Harlem in 1960, Castro met with Malcolm X as large crowds gathered to greet the Cuban leader, while in Cuba huge rallies denounced the racism of the United States. 'To Harlem's oppressed ghetto-dwellers, Castro was that bearded revolutionary who had thrown the nation's rascals out and who had told white America to go to hell,' reported the *New York Citizen Call*, a black newspaper.

This time around, the crowd that stood patiently in line waiting to hear the Cuban leader's September 2000 speech seemed equally as appreciative of Castro's solidarity with black causes. 'Harlem is home for Castro. We love him, he's our brother,' said real estate broker and Harlem native Jabir El-Amin. 'People of African descent have an affinity for him. He believes in true freedom for all peoples, for all Cubans and particularly for Africans and people of African descent. And he has stood steadfast in his beliefs, and kept his dignity and the dignity of his people despite the sanctions and pressures put on his people.'

Hisham Aidi, *www.africana.com*

was invited by Malcolm X to move up to Harlem to stay at the Hotel Theresa. Castro later recalled, 'I immediately decided: "I will go to Harlem because that is where my best friends are."' Castro's first visit to Harlem marked the beginning of a long history of Cuban solidarity with African-America, of a warmth and a sympathy generated between, as Castro put it, two peoples of the third world – the people of Cuba and the people of the third world of the United States.

Bombing Iraq – since 1920

> The West won the world not by the superiority of its ideas or values or religion but rather by its superiority in applying organized violence. Westerners often forget this fact, non-Westerners never do.
>
> Samuel P. Huntington, cited on the 'Where is Raed?' website, a day-to-day journal of everyday life in Baghdad under bombardment

I was standing on the balcony looking out over the skyline of yellow houses towards the dark limestone mountains of the North, which rose steeply into the evening sky. I could still make out the vast flag of Cyprus' Turkish Republic hanging across the mountainside, an enormous mosaic of bright painted stones laid out to make a crescent and star between two horizontal stripes, all red against a white background. Wherever you are in Nicosia, whenever you look North, you see that flag, floating defiantly across the skyline, with its uncompromising message written beside it: 'Ne mutlu turkum diyene' – 'How happy to be a Turk'. It is over 25 years since the island was partitioned. The barbed wire on the United Nations line dividing the two sides is rusty, many of the command and lookout posts seem to have been long deserted. Yet still virtually nothing moves across it; still the two sides stare at each other across walls, wire, and invisible mines of the divide, remembering their abandoned homes, the people in their families still missing, the nights when whole villages were massacred. One more lingering colonial effect that, coming after a hard-won independence struggle, could be safely blamed on the people themselves.

I watched the lingering light fading on the hills, listening to the *adhān al-maghrib*, the evening call to prayer, from the other side of the city. In the background, I could hear the sound of the Reuters emails coming in on the PC inside, as everyone all over the region filed in their evening reports. I looked back at the desk and saw there was a message from Khaled, who had recently been posted to Baghdad. I double-clicked the cursor on his name and his message came up.

From: Khaled   Sent: Wed 22/01/2003 23:08

To: Shayan

Cc:

Subject: Re. Report

Assalam alaikum. I managed to meet up at last tonight with that man I told you about. It was hard to get in touch with everything that was going on at the office, and at his office too, where they're busy trying to move the treasures of the collection to somewhere safer – the Museum is right by the main telephone exchange and the Foreign Ministry. Anyway, eventually we arranged to meet up at Al-Haj-Muhammad's, at the corner of Mustansir St. The conversation took an unexpected turn. Don't send this to the news desk – can you file it to features please? Also, ask Nick if he can get it syndicated. Thanks. K.

'The right to bomb': Baghdad, 21 January 2003

As I walked in, I saw him from the other side of the room, staring abstractedly at the diamond-patterned tiles on the floor, his hands wrapped together at the end of his thin arms. I sat down and he ordered coffee for us both. We spoke warmly of old mutual friends, and of his years in Paris and in London. Sadiq is a senior deputy to the director-general of antiquities in Baghdad, specializing in Mesopotamian books of the Seljuk era (12th–13th centuries CE). Some years ago, he published an impressive scholarly account of Dioscorides' *De Materia Medica* (1224 CE) on the strength of his Ph.D. research, and is now well known as an authority on medical treatises of that era. He spent over a year in Paris studying the *Kitab ad-Diryak* (*The Book of Antidotes*, 1199 CE) at the Bibliothèque

Nationale, and had sent me an article of his in which he analysed the exquisite illustrations in that book of the cultivation of plants for their medicinal properties. I wanted to know much more about the extraordinary role of plants and herbs in medicine at that time, and I began to explain to him why I had come. All of a sudden, the dust rose up from the floor and we heard a dull explosion in the distance. He caught my eye and rolled his tongue round his dry mouth. At first he said nothing, the natural instinct of a man who has survived against the odds through the turbulent, sometimes terrible decades of the regime. His scholarship, safely focused on the glorious artefacts created when Baghdad was the centre of the Islamic world eight centuries ago, has helped him to achieve a certain political invisibility. Then he looked me in the eye again and began to speak.

It's the British again. They have been bombing my family for over 80 years now. Four generations have lived and died with these unwanted visitors from Britain who come to pour explosives on us from the skies. It first began in 1920. My great grandfather, Abd Al Rahman, was walking into our village for his last-born son's wedding when a two-winged plane suddenly came over the horizon and dropped a fireball amongst the celebrations. The guests were divided into separate areas for men and women, as they used to be in the villages in those days. The bomb fell on the men gathered inside, and killed or maimed half the men in our family – the first-born son, three uncles, two cousins, four sons of my grandmother's father's brother. Since then, whenever it has suited them, the bombers come again.

Now their big brothers from America do most of it, but you can still see the RAF planes streaking across our skies flying their familiar routes, which they first charted in the 1920s. The flights began in earnest when they were preparing to leave finally (again) after the Second World War. They mapped every metre of our territory, laboriously, meticulously, took photographs of every square centimetre of our country. My cousin who studied there told me that at Keele University in England there are millions of reconnaissance photographs on microfilm of Iraq and Iran taken by RAF 680 squadron before they left. You never know when we might need them, they said with a smile. When they look for oil, or decide to bomb us when they want to make sure they will have more of our oil for the future. Probably they still use them today when they sit in their operation rooms in England and plan which target amongst us to hit next.

Every square centimetre of our country photographed, from Al Basrah on the Gulf to Amādīyah in the mountains to the north. Our country! In a sense, though, it has hardly been our country at all – even if it has always been our land. Like most of the states in the Middle East it was invented by two men, one French, one English, during the First World War. Georges Sykes and Sir Mark Picot, they were called. You know, they just met up in London and decided in secret between the two of them how it would all be. The defeated Ottoman Empire would be dismembered, and new countries – Palestine, Transjordan, Iraq, Syria, Lebanon' – simply invented out of the bits for the convenience of the two colonial powers that would rule them. The British, of course, already controlled Egypt and Sudan. Iraq was made out of three leftover *vilayat* (provinces) of the Ottoman Empire. In 1920, they said they would give the Kurds an independent state, Kurdistan; in 1923, they just forgot all about it, according to the whim of the moment. They created states that were no nations, just sets of lines drawn on the map according to their interests. There had been no borders or boundaries between us all. The whole of the Empire was open from one end to the other. There were different regions, of course, ours was Upper and Lower Mesopotamia, as it always had been. Then their boundaries, drawn in the fluid sand with their barbed wire, marked out their new 'protectorates', empty they said except for a few nameless tribesmen like my great grandfather and grandfather who did not need to be consulted about what was good for them. Nomads have no rights. They are not really there at all.

Not like the oil company that came quickly afterwards. Or the soldiers. Those French quickly landed their Senegalese troops in Beirut when the war ended and occupied the whole northern coastal area. The British, with their Indian troops, controlled Palestine, put in advisers elsewhere in Syria, and occupied the whole of Mesopotamia. All their Middle Eastern colonies in those days were run by Anglo-Indian administrations. They were not British colonies you know – they were 'dependencies of British India'.

He stopped for a moment, looked hard at the floor, and fell into silence. I offered him a cigarette. He smoked it for a while, watching the blue smoke rise to the ceiling.

'So what happened then?' I asked. 'After they had taken over?' He breathed hard, and shook his head.

Well. Between the two of them, they occupied the whole of the old territories of the Empire. At the same time, the British made several public statements to international forums that all 'liberated' territories would be governed on the principle of what they called the 'consent of the governed', by their own national administrations. The Arabs took them at their word: had they not already been induced to fight with the British against the Turks on that very promise? Remember that so-called Lawrence of Arabia they still make so much of. So, in March 1920, the General Syrian Congress in Damascus passed a resolution proclaiming independence for Syria, Palestine, and the Lebanon. Iraqi leaders immediately declared Iraq's independence too, with Amir Abdullah their king. Those British and French responded by going straight to the League of Nations, which obligingly gave them mandates over the whole territory. Not surprising, since they controlled it anyway. Mandate from whom? They said themselves that the term 'mandate' was just a piece of legal fiction to legitimate their new colonies.

We didn't just accept it all, though. King Faisal's troops attacked the French on the Lebanon border, the Arabs rose against the Jews in

Palestine, and our people of the Middle Euphrates rose against the British. The French responded by occupying the whole of Syria. In Iraq, the British did not use their Indian troops: instead they used the newly formed Royal Air Force to bomb us. My great grandfather's wedding, remember? They had already used the RAF in Somaliland. In a two-month joint operation with the British Camel Corps they had overthrown the Dervish leader Mohammed bin Abdullah Hassan – whom the British characteristically just called the 'Mad Mullah'. Mad because he wanted to get rid of them, of course. It was generally thought that the air force bombing and strafing against the nationalists had been the key to the operation's success.

Their new colonial secretary, Winston Churchill, he recognized early on the advantages of airpower for maintaining imperial control over his vast British territories. Before the uprising had even begun, he had enquired about the possibility of using airpower to take control of Iraq. This would involve, he said, using 'some kind of asphyxiating bombs calculated to cause disablement of some kind but not death . . . for use in preliminary operations against turbulent tribes'. You can't forget words like that. Nor the ones that followed. 'I do not understand this squeamishness about the use of gas', he said. 'I am strongly in favour of using poison gas against uncivilized tribes.' So, after the Somaliland success, Churchill ordered a similar RAF operation in Iraq. The result was predictable. The rebellious Iraqis were also successfully 'pacified'. They made war and called it peace. Does it make any difference for them? Churchill came to Cairo the next year, with his Lawrence of Arabia, for a conference on the future of the British mandates. No Arabs were invited. They installed Faisal, whom the French had thrown out of Syria, as King of Iraq. Despite fierce resistance in Baghdad, a plebiscite was arranged to vote him in.

Yes, the new RAF had been out to prove its use. It had only just been set up as a separate section of their armed forces. Anyone could see the advantages of technology like that for controlling far-away peoples. Wing-Commander Sir Arthur Harris, that notorious 'Bomber Harris', put it this way: 'The Arab and Kurd now know what real bombing means in casualties and damage. Within 45 minutes a full-size village can be practically wiped out and a third of its inhabitants killed or injured.' Just 45 minutes a village – not bad. So the British established five RAF squadrons in Britain, five in Egypt, four in Iraq and in India, and one in the Far East. From now on we would never see their faces when we were fighting. Yes, after they had got rid of the Turks, when some of us had fought alongside them, they returned from the air like demons. For months RAF 30 Squadron flew over us, killing our men and our families until it was safe for the Indian soldiers and their British officers to set up their camps nearby. British control was restored.

I still have one of the propaganda photographs they produced at the time of our first 'liberation' from the Turks. It's a picture of the 'Peace Review'. This Peace Review was just the first, for another defeat and triumph followed – this time that of the British over the Iraqis. Look at that de Havilland 9 flying overhead, with its machine-gunner facing backwards ready to spray bullets on anyone below, with its 450 pounds of bombs tucked beneath its wings. Doesn't leave you many illusions about who is in charge. Power comes from above. Look.

He rummaged in his briefcase, took out an old, dog-eared postcard, and handed it to me. I peered at it for a while, trying to make it all out. From the shadows, it must have been evening. A big circle of Arab spectators was watching a military parade. In the centre, British officers were standing opposite a line of ranked Camel Corps. Huge flags were flapping above them, while an old two-winged aircraft was flying prominently overhead. I could make out the French flag and the Union Jack.

'What's the flag at the front?' I asked.

8. Peace review, Baghdad, 1918.

It's the Italian navy ensign. They fought on the side of the British in that war, remember. Keep it! A souvenir, for you, to remember all this when you leave. They will only stay a while, my grandfather had heard. Indeed, they did go away eventually, in 1932, but as in Egypt, this did not mean that we became really independent. Some independence! We were made to sign a treaty in which we agreed to let Britain control our foreign policy, keep its two air bases at Habbaniyya near Baghdad and Shu'aiba near Basra, use Iraq freely for its troops in time of war, and maintain its complete monopoly of the Iraq Petroleum Company. It may have been called the Iraq Petroleum Company, but the British government controlled it. There was no Iraqi ownership at all. According to the independence treaty, the IPC was given exclusive exploration rights in Iraq. These were revoked in 1961, but the company itself did not come under Iraqi control until it was nationalized by Hasan al-Bakr and Saddam Hussein in 1972. That was a popular move. No wonder they don't like him! They want to get their oil back. They are already talking about which of their companies will get the rights to it when they have occupied our country again.

He smiled for a moment, and then sunk back into his chair as if he was thinking ahead to the prospect of another occupation. He had stopped looking at me, and was going over it all in his mind, as if it was a story that once started, he could not stop himself from telling right through to the end, however many times he would have to backtrack and retrace the pattern of its compulsive, sinuous repetitions.

So the British left, but only in name. We were to govern ourselves, we were told, under their guidance and control. Things came to a head during the Second World War, when many of us looked to the Axis powers to deliver us from submission to Britain. When Prime Minister Rashid 'Ali al-Kailani got a bit awkward about giving permission for British troops to land in Iraq, they made it known that he would have to go, and he was forced to resign. Rashid 'Ali responded by organizing a *coup d'état* against the anglophile Prince

Regent. The British refused to recognize his government, and demanded their right to more troop landings. Their commander at Habbaniyya then attacked Iraqi troops that had surrounded the base. Soon they occupied Basra, took Baghdad, and reinstated the Prince Regent on the throne. Their brute force had won control once more. Directed by the British Embassy, the new regime instituted a purge of the armed forces and government administration, and sent nationalist sympathizers for execution or to the Al-Faw detention camp. That's where they put my father, Abu Karim. He was in there all the time I was growing up as a young boy.

That cosy relationship between the British and their tame Iraqi dynasty (just like the one they had with the Shah of Persia and the King of Jordan, whom they'd also put on their thrones) continued right up to the Baghdad Pact in 1955, the last fawning agreement of a Hashemite monarch with the British. The next year it was Suez! The British were beaten! And before long, in 1958, there was a second army *coup d'état*, which brought the end of the hated Hashemite regime, and with it the end of British influence in Iraq. But not the end of British intervention. At first we thought we had seen the last of them. No tame monarchy, no bases, no canal, but still getting the oil they wanted. Why would they ever come back? They had left with their tails between their legs, and the freed world had asserted itself at Bandung. But then they lost Iran, and Saddam was encouraged to take them out. We were dying again. They were back.

Now they are saying that we are 'a threat' to them. But hasn't it always been they who have threatened us? Oh yes, they certainly constitute a threat to us. They have been developing nuclear weapons since the 1940s. They were bombing us with chemicals long before then. It was Churchill himself who ordered the use of mustard gas against the Kurds in Northern Iraq in 1923, when they rebelled on hearing that the British had abandoned their promise of a Kurdish state. It took almost a year and a half of repeated RAF attacks on the Kurdish city of Sulaimaniyya before they were finally repressed. Well, hardly finally. The RAF was bombing the Kurds again in 1931 when the British were preparing Iraq for 'independence', which they were about to grant without any reference to the special position of the Kurds in Iraq. You can still meet Kurds today who can remember being machine-gunned and bombed by the RAF in the 1920s. My friend Ibrahim was visiting the Korak mountains a while ago and came across an old man who could still recall it all. 'They were bombing here in the Kaniya Khoran', he told him. 'Sometimes they raided three times a day.'

Of course, it's the Iraqis who are branded 'irresponsible'. After all, didn't Saddam invade Kuwait? Well, that was a mistake, though of course many of us Iraqis do feel strongly that historically Kuwait has always been part of Iraq. Anyway, you know very well how the Allies quickly mobilized in 1992 to restore Kuwait's sovereignty and reclaim their oil. 'How come they didn't do the same for the Occupied Territories?', people asked. Only a few amongst us were old enough to remember the stories of how in 1920 British planes and armoured cars had been mobilized against the Saudi kabals, 'tribes', who were invading Britain's new 'sovereign' territories of Iraq and Transjordan. The British then gave a large part of Saudi territory to the new state of Iraq, and in compensation they handed over to Ibn Saud, Sultan of Nejd (Saudi Arabia, that is) – yes, they gave him two-thirds of Kuwait.

When the British government was practising that kind of arbitrary territorial fluidity, the Iraqi claim to the remainder was inevitable. Kuwait had, after all, originally been a part of the Ottoman province out of which Iraq was created, and without it, our access to the waters of the Gulf was made almost impossible. The British themselves took the strip of land between Maan and Aqaba from Ibn Saud in 1924, on the grounds that it had once formed part of the Ottoman province of Damascus and therefore ought to be part of Palestine. So it was the British who set up the authority of the argument. It was their Hashemite monarch, King Ghazi, who in the late 1930s first championed Iraq's claim to Kuwait, which at that time was a British colony, on the same grounds. The British, though, had signed a treaty of protection with the Sheikh of Kuwait as early as 1899, which is why, on the break-up of the Ottoman Empire, it was created as a separate puppet state and separated from the Ottoman province of Basra to which it had belonged. When the Iraqi general 'Abd al-Karim Qasim once again made a claim to Kuwait on its independence from Britain in 1961, the British immediately responded by landing troops. Thirty years later they would be back. The bombs would begin again.

Yes, we are a threat to them. Every time we break bread, thousands of them are at risk from each munch of our teeth. Every time I chew a grape or a sugared date, suck a mulberry or an apricot, someone in England must shudder in fear. Every time my son climbs a tree to find a fig, the fine imperial gentlemen of England are put at risk. Yet all we have ever wanted to do is to live our own lives without them. The other night on TV I heard an old Iraqi layman saying, 'They have everything, we have nothing. We don't want anything from them – but they still want more from us'. All we ask is for them to stop interfering with us. We have not been bombing them since 1920. It is they who have been bombing us. Do they never think of that? It never bothers them. They seem to think of it as their god-given right. Or is it another of their human rights – the right to bomb? Not by our God, *alhamdo lillah*. Bombing us ever since their air force was formed, whenever they chose. And still they claim that it is we who are a threat to them. So much so that they have been killing us over the decades, bomb after bomb after bomb, whenever we displeased them or went against their interests. Our problem, though, I suppose, is that we have never been an easy catch. We didn't just go along with everything they wanted, like some countries in the Middle East. So they keep coming and bombing, but we keep slipping out of their grasp, again and again! They will never subdue us, you will see, never 'pacify' us – even if they keep at it for all eternity.

It was a few years ago, in 1998, two days before Ramadan. My family were all sleeping in our flat in Baghdad, in the high apartment building that looks down Mansur St, towards Zawra' Park. A couple of hours before we were to rise for the early-morning prayer, the *fajr*, the sirens suddenly sounded and bombs began to fall around us, lighting the sky with their sinister firework explosions. The white powdery fronts of buildings and bridges were dropping away like sandcastles collapsing before the tide. Since then, and their invention of their 'no-fly zones', they have never really stopped. Except for when they vanish so that the Turks can fly in and bomb the Kurds – the very people that their no-fly zone is supposed to be protecting. The British themselves admit that they have bombed us at least once every other day over the past year. It is their longest bombing campaign since the Second World War. Now they say they are coming again, to destroy our families once more and to change our government just as they did so many times before. Why do they come out of the skies at us for so many years from so far away? Why are we of such interest to them? Because we have 'their' oil. That is the real threat that has never gone away, from 1920 until today.

I often wonder how they would feel if we had been bombing them in England every now and then from one generation to the next, if we changed their governments when it suited us, destroyed their hospitals, made sure they had no clean water, and killed their children and their families. How many children is it that have died now? I can't even bring myself to think how many. They say that their imperial era is over now. It does not feel that way when you hear the staccato crack of their fireballs from the air. Or when the building shakes around you and your children from their bombs as you lie in your bed. It is then that you dream of real freedom – *in shaa' allah* – freedom from the RAF.

Chapter 3
Space and land

Landlessness: 'Morte e vida severina'

According to the Oxford English Dictionary, the term landlessness
has only been written once in English, by Herman Melville in 1851,
when he wrote: 'In landlessness alone resides the highest truth'.
Not an Anglo-Saxon problem, therefore, it would seem. For other
societies, however, many other societies, in fact, including some of
those living in Anglo-Saxon countries, the problem of landlessness
is one of the most immediate and significant issues faced every day
by ordinary people. In many colonized countries, settlers created
vast farms and estates by driving off those who had traditionally
lived on that land, some of whose descendants continue to this day
to live in an impoverished landless limbo. Without land to cultivate,
the only alternative is to drift to the slums of the big cities. Even the
sanctuary of the slum is itself vulnerable, as in apartheid South
Africa, or contemporary Mumbai.

Take Brazil, for example – a country which has the ninth-largest
gross national product in the world but which also holds the world
record for the country with the most unequal distribution of
income. It is a country where 3% of the population own two-thirds
of cultivable land, and in which 60% of the land lies idle. The
deprivation of people living in such conditions, particularly in the
state of Recife, the poorest in Brazil, has produced many rebellions,

9. Maria da Silva stands with four of the eight children who live with her and her husband Valdemar in Nova Canudos, the squatter camp set up by the Landless Workers' Movement in Anhembi, 130 miles from Sao Paulo, Brazil, 30 July 1999.

peasant leagues, revolutionary impulses, and guerrilla movements. More recently, a different political response has developed: the *Movimento Sem Terra* (Movement of Landless Rural Workers). Faced with the vast estates, *latifundia*, held by a tiny minority of landowners, the *Movimento Sem Terra* (MST) not only campaigns against the injustice of this situation, but, with a slogan of 'Occupy, Resist, and Produce', encourages the 12 million landless workers in Brazil to occupy uncultivated areas of land. The MST is one of the largest grassroots organizations in the world, and today, after MST land takeovers, more than 250,000 families have won land titles to over 15 million acres. Many more thousands of families are awaiting official recognition of their settlements. In the meantime, there have been often violent clashes between peasant farmers, landowners, and police.

The MST always works on a principle of collectivity and

community. from the first, the MST established food cooperatives, primary schools, and literacy programmes in their settlements. All farms are run with respect for environmental issues: the MST produces the only organic seeds in Latin America. The MST also places great emphasis on health care, seen from a holistic perspective in which health involves not just a question of access to medicines and clinics, but is also concerned with the environment, hygiene, and the well-being of everyone in society. This concept of health includes a person's social environment: as the MST puts it:

> Thus, health is how and where you live, what you eat, and how you make a living. It is feeling well physically, being mentally at peace, living in a family setting where there is respect, affection, and equality among all, respecting nature, and living in a society in which justice and equality go hand in hand.

What is remarkable is not just that this is a politics of health that any postcolonial activist would be proud to share. It is also that the MST sees it as part of its goal to develop such a holistic view of the life of the people who make up its communities.

In 1997, in an attempt to regain the political initiative and control land reform through the traditional channels of power, and with $150 million of special aid provided by the World Bank, the Brazilian government challenged the MST by initiating an alternative 'market-based' land reform programme, known as 'Cedula da Terra'. The scheme involves lending money at high rates of interest to the landless to buy land; it is administered by local regional councils who work with the landowners. The programme has been widely criticized as an example of the World Bank intervening in domestic politics on the side of the landowners. Opposition to it, however, has enabled the MST to go from strength to strength. A significant sign of the unintended effects of World Bank intervention in Brazilian politics came with the election of Luiz Inácio da Silva – known to everyone as Lula – as president of Brazil in November 2002. Born into extreme poverty in Recife, Lula never got past elementary school but then rose to become a trade union leader and founder of the Workers' Party. He greeted the news of his election with an announcement in which he made clear his political priorities:

> My first year will focus on combating hunger. It's an appeal of solidarity with the Brazilians who have nothing to eat.

In many ways, the MST figures as a model for a postcolonial politics: a grassroots movement formed to fight a system of injustice and gross material inequality that is sustained by powerful local interests and international power structures of banks, businesses, and investment funds that want to maintain the status quo of the global economic market. The movement is organized on a collective basis on behalf of the well-being of ordinary people, and, as we have seen, extends its care from the appropriation of land to wide social issues including the status of women, the well-being of children, health care, education, and the promotion of a healthy environment. In this way, the MST must work at a local level: but encountering its opponents not only amongst the landowners, and in local and national government, but also directly in the World Bank means that it must also consider a larger perspective, and fight for its arguments on a wide range of platforms and in public spaces. It is for this reason that movements such as MST link up with comparable peasant movements in other countries – such as the *Kilusang Magbubukid ng Pilipinas* (KMP), a nationwide federation of Philippine organizations of landless peasants, small farmers, farm workers, subsistence fishermen, peasant women, and rural youth – as well as with larger global social movements – such as People's Global Action (PGA), a broad alliance of resistance movements that campaign against the forcibly imposed inequalities of the World Trade Organization (WTO). The PGA's 'Global Action Days', intended to highlight resistance to a globalized capitalism and 'the dictatorship of the markets' and organized in Geneva, Seattle, and Prague at meetings of the WTO, G8, and World Bank, have been highly successful in bypassing the conventional channels according to which it would fall to representatives of their own governments to intervene on their behalf. Since third-world governments appear powerless to intervene against the interests of the G8 powers, the PGA has taken direct populist action which has already achieved considerable impact.

The MST also works alongside tribal movements in which native peoples, such as the Guarani, Makuxi, and Xucuru in Brazil, are attempting to reassert their rights to land that has been taken from them by ranchers and goldminers. The problem of landlessness remains central to the politics of many millions across the world, and has long been the main focus of much political opposition and peasant unrest amongst those who make up the wretched of the earth. In Mexico, the current Zapatista movement works in a line of direct continuity that goes back to the 1910 Zapatista revolution of the peasantry against the big landowners, the *hacendados*, who had expropriated their land. The South Africa Native Land Act of 1913 made it illegal for African people to possess or occupy land outside the 'Scheduled Native Areas', except as farm labourers. As a result, many lost their homes and means of subsistence. In India, peasant or tribal movements and rebellions, and acts of resistance against the *zamindari* landholding system, have continued uninterrupted from the colonial to the independence period, from the Gandhian Kisan peasant movement to the Maoist Naxalites.

The experience of dispossession and landlessness is also typical of settler colonialism, and is historically most difficult to resolve. It was in 1972 that Aborigines and Torres Strait Islanders established their famous 'Tent Embassy', a tin shack on the lawns of Capital Hill in Canberra, as a highly effective strategy to publicize their claim for land rights. The struggle for 'native title' has also been a major concern for native Americans in North America, for aboriginals in India, and for the dispossessed African farmers in Zimbabwe who have campaigned for the basic land rights embodied in the Abuja Declaration, while dispossession from family land and the claim for the right of return represents the central issue in Palestine.

These are all postcolonial struggles, typically dealing with the aftermath of one of the most banal but fundamentally important features of colonial power: the appropriation of land. It is striking that the so-called 'agrarian question', which cut little ice with western revolutionaries, was always a major political theme for those with a tricontinental perspective – Mao, Fanon, Guevara,

This toiling humanity, inhumanly exploited, these paupers, controlled by the whip and overseer, have not reckoned with or have been little reckoned with. From the dawn of independence their fate has been the same: Indians, gauchos, mestizos, zambos, quadroons, whites without property or income, all this human mass which formed the ranks of the 'nation', which never reaped any benefits ... which continued to die of hunger, curable diseases and neglect, because for them there were never enough essentials of life – ordinary bread, a hospital bed, the medicine which cures, the hand which aids – their fate has been all the same.

But now ... this anonymous mass, this America of colour, sombre, taciturn America, which all over the continent sings with the same sadness and disillusionment, now this mass is beginning to enter conclusively into its own history, is beginning to write it with its own blood, is beginning to suffer and die for it ...

Yes, now history will have to take the poor of America into account, the exploited and spurned of Latin America, who have decided to begin writing history for themselves for all time.

'Second Declaration of Havana', The People of Cuba, Havana, Cuba, Free Territory of America, 4 February 1962

Subcommandante Marcos. To think about landlessness is to think about the peasantry and the whole spectrum of needs of the world's poorest people. It is doubtless a mark of the present state of things that today we think of the landless peasant rather than the 1960s figure of the rural guerrilla. Either way, the necessity of agrarian reform has always been central for the continuing revolutionary peasant movements, from Columbia to Peru, from Nepal to Assam.

Nomads

> The colonial state in South Asia was very unlike and indeed fundamentally different from the metropolitan bourgeois state which had sired it. The difference consisted in the fact that the metropolitan state was hegemonic in character with its claim to dominance based on a power relation in which the moment of persuasion outweighed that of coercion, whereas the colonial state was non-hegemonic with persuasion outweighed by coercion in its structure of dominance ... And since it was non-hegemonic, it was not possible for that state to assimilate the civil society of the colonized to itself. We have defined the character of the colonial state therefore as a *dominance without hegemony*.
>
> Ranajit Guha, *Dominance without Hegemony* (1997)

The concept of landlessness implies a person who has become landless, exiled from their land. Landless means land loss, land lost. 'Becoming' landless depends on your relation to the land. Nomadic people were never in possession of the land in a European sense, which is how colonists were able, following the 17th-century English philosopher John Locke, to declare the land empty, '*terra nulla*'. It is for this reason that 'native title' represents a claim of extraordinary complexity. At war, here, are not simply two different peoples but also epistemologies, where the European, as the critic and legal historian Eric Cheyfitz has so effectively shown, brings with him and her a notion of property and the proper, of ownership and possession, that are fundamentally at odds with those who cannot be assimilated into such a system. The nomad works the land, has an intimate relation to the land, but does not affiliate him- or herself to it in a relation of property or ownership. The relationship is rather a sacred and ancestral one.

The French philosophers Gilles Deleuze and Félix Guattari have conceptualized the process of the appropriation of land and its confiscation from those who have formerly worked it, with or without legal title, through the concepts of what they call 'territorialization' and 'deterritorialization'. A third moment of 'reterritorialization' describes the violent dynamics of the colonial or imperial propagation of economic, cultural, and social transformation of the indigenous culture, at the same time as characterizing the successful process of resistance to deterritorialization through the anti-colonial movements. Other forms of resistance have developed in the postcolonial state: combative negotiation with the state, as in the case of the MST, or even, as is happening in the American Midwest, the simple repurchase of lands which were appropriated as part of the homesteading colonization of the land by settlers in the 19th century, but which are now being abandoned as virtually worthless, in part because of the slump in farming, in part because the land itself is not as fertile for intensive agriculture as the American government had originally assumed.

Deleuze and Guattari have further developed the idea of the nomad as a strategic concept, arguing that the nomad is the person who most effectively resists the controlling institutions of the state. Any account of gypsies or 'travellers' in Europe, from Spain to Switzerland, will provide graphic instances of the ways in which, for the past hundred years, the state has regarded those whose life involves a permanent state of migrancy as a serious threat that requires heavy-handed intervention, stabilization, and control.

The idea of nomadism, Deleuze and Guattari argue, can be extended to include all forms of cultural and political activity that transgress or dissolve the boundaries of contemporary social codes. Less metaphorically, nomadism involves the practice of movement across territories, operating as lateral resistance across borders in acts of defiance of assertions of hegemonic control. 'Terrorism', now being rapidly codified as operating through transnational networks, would be an extreme example of the characteristic political activity that such nomadism involves. Landlessness reminds us, however, that nomadism cannot be celebrated simply as an anti-capitalist strategy, for the simple reason that nomadism is rather one brutal characteristic mode of capitalism itself. The history of capitalism has involved the closure of land and the resulting enforced movement of its inhabitants to the only available, if available, work in the cities. In anti-colonial and postcolonial history, nomads have not just been those who still live in a precapitalist mode of subsistence: in the past two centuries, nomadism has been the state of existence forced upon millions. Landlessness constitutes the central problem for many peasant communities around the world, as well as for the world's 20 million refugees, who have no land in a material sense, but are also landless in terms of their own state – stateless, homeless, without a land.

Some western postmodernists have tried to characterize nomadism and migration as examples of the most productive forms of cultural identity, emphasizing the creative performativity of identity, as opposed to an identity derived from the physical affiliations of family and place. This may be all very well for cosmopolitan intellectuals. But how could this postmodern 'migratory' identity be celebrated in the refugee camps of Qetta, Jalozai, and elsewhere in Pakistan, with their 2.5 million Afghan refugees (about 12% of all the world's refugees), in the West Bank, in the former Sangatte camp in France? How can a migratory identity be celebrated by the

460 mainly Afghan refugees who were cooped up for eight days on a Norwegian cargo ship, the *Tampa*, having been refused permission to land by the Australian government, and then sent to the tiny, barren Pacific island of Nauru, the world's smallest republic, a 300-metre strip of palm trees and disused phosphate mines, where they landed, each carrying one black plastic bin liner containing their possessions? The Australians have given Nauru about A\$15 million in order to avoid admitting the 460 refugees into Australia (which works out at about A\$360,000 a person).

Perhaps they were the lucky ones. At least they were not imprisoned in Australia's notorious Woomera Detention Centre, which is located 300 miles from the nearest city in the middle of the desert, and is subject to daytime temperatures of up to 42 degrees Celsius. In January 2002, hundreds of Afghan refugees who had been sent there went on hunger strike. At least 70 of them began sewing up their lips to draw attention to their plight. Others, including children, attempted simultaneous suicide. A 12-year-old girl told investigators,

> I am getting crazy, I cut my hand. I can't talk to my mother. I can't talk to anyone and I am very tired. There is no solution for me – I just have to commit suicide – there is no choice.

The detention centre at Woomera is run by Australasian Correctional Management Ltd, an offshoot of US-based Wackenhut Corrections Corporation.

Humans, caught in a cave

'We'll smoke 'em out.'
George Bush on the American pursuit of al-Qaeda in Afghanistan

1840: Paris

Theatregoers are flocking to enjoy a new performance of Corneille's *L'illusion comique* at the *Comédie Française*. It is a play very much indebted to Shakespeare's *The Tempest*, transposing the action from a Caribbean island to a cave somewhere in France. Corneille is invoking Plato's famous image invented to illustrate his argument that all that we see on earth, material reality, is in fact an illusion covering or masking the ideal world beyond. To illustrate his point, Plato invokes the analogy of humans standing in a cave. They stand with their backs to the reality of the world outside, and what they believe to be real is really only the shifting, subdued reflection of the real world outside on the cave wall. In *L'illusion comique* Corneille used the analogy for comic effect; the stage becomes the cave, and the audience the real. Or is it vice versa? The main character Pridamant is fooled by a spectral illusion shown to him by Alcandre the musician, in which he sees his lost son as a rich man, dressed like a prince: to Pridamant's horror, however, in the final act he finds himself watching his son being murdered. In the depth of despair, he is then shown his son apparently alive again, dividing up a pile of gold with his murderers. In fact, Alcandre tells him, his son is not a wealthy prince but an actor and what he has been watching has been his performance in a play. The audience leave the theatre amused and tickled by Corneille's evident mastery in staging such a self-conscious yet convincing hall-of-mirrors illusion of the real. They have been equally fooled! The magic aesthetics of the theatre, the creative power of the imagination and its ability to make the real and the illusion interchangeable, have been memorably demonstrated to the audience as they return home to their comfortable houses and apartments across Paris. In their dreams, they relish the power of their poetic imaginations, the airy pageants of Prospero, 'a spectacle to which there is no end'.

1840: 900 miles south of Paris, in the countryside south of Algiers

They move slowly in a line of flight across invisible desert paths, their ankles torn red by the tiny spikes of the stunted bushes in the scrub, then blanched again by the dust of the sand. They climb up through the steep gorges, and then finally find the cave. They walk quickly inside. Its darkness enfolds each one of them, its dampness steams in their nostrils as they breathe in the cold air. Their eyes accustom to the dark, and they begin to make out glints and gleams in the gloom. The surfaces glimmer and glisten, and haunting shapes begin to form before their eyes. The dark, cold cave feels damp, but there is no apparent source of water. Their throats are parched with sharp, stabbing pains. Some walk in deeper in search of moisture, sure that somewhere they can hear a faint ringing of slow drips. Others move back nervously to the entrance, scanning the horizon for movement, their eyes alternately moving downwards over the land and then raised to the sky. There is nothing, no noise except the strong wind and the thrashing of the loose scrub. They move back inside, and find the others making a fire and a place to lie down. Some are already asleep.

When they wake, it is still dark. It is so dark, they cannot see. They begin to smell fresh smoke, and the air becomes increasingly acrid. The oldest man gets up and walks to the entrance. He walks forward, but he cannot find the exit. He scrambles over rubble that is now lying on the floor. He climbs to the top and finds his head against the roof. The entrance to the cave has been blocked up, the smoke is pouring in through the rocks like waves of water, heavy and thick. Asphyxiation is slow. The eyes smart, the lungs pant for breath, which only brings them more acrid, burning smoke.

General Bugeaud is in charge of the task of subduing Algeria. Ten years after the French first invaded, it still requires pacification. Bugeaud's method is *razzia*, scorched earth, slash and burn. Anyone who resists, or is suspected of resisting, is killed. Today he has pursued a group of troublesome tribesmen up into a cave. He seals it up, and then asphyxiates those inside with smoke. He writes in his journal:

> I have all the exits hermetically sealed and I make a huge cemetery. The earth will cover the corpses of these fanatics for all time. No one went down into the caves; no one . . . other than myself knows that

there are 500 brigands under there who will no longer cut the throat of Frenchmen.

By the 1950s, a century later, little had changed since the days of Bugeaud. During the war of independence, the French would still be cheerfully burying Algerians alive, this time by pushing earth on top of them with bulldozers.

2002: Afghanistan

There is a report on the BBC news webpage that American forces in Afghanistan have come up against heavy resistance:

Saturday, 2 March, 2002, 23:42 GMT

Afghan caves hit with pressure bombs

The US forces have dropped two devastating high-pressure blast bombs on suspected Taleban and al–Qaeda positions in the mountains of eastern Afghanistan after a ground offensive ran into difficulty.

US defence sources said two 2,000-pound (907-kg) 'thermobaric' bombs, which send suffocating blasts through cave complexes, were aimed at mountain caves where enemy fighters were hiding.

Thermobaric bombs were tested by the US in December and officials said in January that they would be rushed to Afghanistan for the campaign to root out supporters of Saudi-born dissident Osama Bin Laden.

Laser-guided, it is filled with a special explosive mixture that creates a high-pressure blast, driving all of the air out of a cave and potentially choking those inside.

Russia has used similar fuel-air bombs in Chechnya, causing international protests.

'A spectacle to which there is no end'

From 1840 to the present, then, the cave has often been the site of western intervention against the peoples of the Islamic world: 'A spectacle to which there is no end'. This burying, this suppression, this suffocation, literally sucking the air out of the lungs of men, women, and children, becomes a metaphor for the suppression of the colonized world itself – the air that it breathes sucked out in the moment that the west likes to describe innocuously as 'the colonial encounter': now the memory and memorial of asphyxiation and colonial violence.

Meanwhile, westerners carry on going to the theatre. Art and politics don't mix, they always say. The very division of the world on which aesthetics rests is a product of the Manichean, or dualistic, colonial, patriarchal mentality isolated by the revolutionary psychologist Frantz Fanon at the opening of his *The Wretched of the Earth* (1961). Through their 'aesthetic expressions of respect for the established order', says Fanon, 'in the capitalist countries a multitude of moral teachers, professors, counsellors and "disorientators" (*désorientateurs*, literally, bewilderers) separate the exploited from those in power'. As an intellectual, an artist, a consumer or producer of culture, you either collude with the aestheticized structure that enforces apartness, or you contest it – by turning the theatre into a site of resistance, for example.

The recognition of these sorts of disjunctions, the articulation of the aesthetic life of the west with the brutal military power that has sustained its wealth and interests; the recognition that, from a different perspective, caves may not necessarily involve the imaginative excitement of *King Solomon's Mines* (1885), or even the spiritual and sexual cultural confusion of the Marabar Caves in *A Passage to India* (1924), but reek with the memory of asphyxiation and colonial violence: all this represents the fundamental reorientation involved in postcolonial critique. The death of Katharine at the end of Michael Ondaatje's *The English Patient*

(1992) stages this dissonance in reverse: beneath the sublime
aesthetics of the ancient figure paintings that adorn the walls of
the Cave of Swimmers in the Gilf Kebir at Uweinat, the English
woman lies dying, wrapped in a parachute in the cold darkness, the
victim of the brutal European war being played out in the desert all
around her.

> What I am interested in doing now is suggesting how the
> general liberal consensus that 'true' knowledge is funda-
> mentally non-political (and conversely, that overtly political
> knowledge is not 'true' knowledge) obscures the highly if
> obscurely organized political circumstances obtaining when
> knowledge is produced. No one is helped in understanding
> this today when the adjective 'political' is used as a label to
> discredit any work for daring to violate the protocol of
> pretended suprapolitical objectivity.
>
> Edward W. Said, *Orientalism* (1978)

Unsettled states: nations and their borders

> The government of India states that 'the external boundaries
> of India are neither correct nor authenticated'.
>
> Legend on all maps of India

Does anything really make up a nation apart from its borders?
There are 'nations' without physical borders: the first nations of
Canada (a title chosen by indigenous North Americans for
themselves, in preference to the usual term 'fourth world'), the
'Nation of Islam', although it could be said the Nation polices its
own borders with some care. The border creates the limit of the

nation, and produces the space in which the nation's infrastructional machinery, its government, its tax collectors, can operate. The nation is a kind of corporation. It is the border that allows another nation to recognize it as a nation, to send its representatives there, so that it can participate in the global community of nations. A community without communal values.

The territory of the earth is a mosaic of nations: or is it simply a mosaic of states? What makes a state a nation? Does it need to be one? The problem for the state, unless it possesses a monarch endowed with divine authority, is the question of what legitimates its authority. As the French discovered in 1789, the idea of the nation fulfils this function in an ideal way. As a larger corporation, to which its citizens necessarily belong without choice, the nation becomes an empty space in which all forms of potential identification can be filled: race, religion, language, culture, history, the land: what makes you a part of your nation?

It always used to be assumed that in order to become a nation, the people of a nation should resemble each other as closely as possible. If they looked different, spoke a different language, followed a different religion, then this was considered a threat to what the political theorist Benedict Anderson has characterized as the 'imagined community' of the nation. Many people, languages, cultures, have been repressed for this reason. The United States, a nation of immigrants, makes an interesting test case in its attempt to deal with this problem of how to make the many one. First of all, everyone in the US has something in common, that they or their ancestors came as immigrants – though awkwardly this does not apply to the first nations of native Americans who were displaced or exterminated in order to make room for the new arrivals. Secondly, unlike most countries, more like an old dynastic empire in fact, even the landmass of the US is not attached, but dispersed with other countries and oceans in between (this is probably not why Americans use the term 'the world' to mean the US, as in the so-called World Series). The absence of traditional links to land, history, and culture explains why the US has to make an identity for itself out of its liberal state ideology (democracy, liberty, free enterprise capitalism), and why it has to create demonic enemies which are alleged to threaten its very existence (successively: witchcraft, Chinese immigrants, communism, Hispanics who won't speak the state's official language English, African-Americans who speak Ebonics, African killer bees, Islam . . .). These enemies serve to make all its different people feel collectively threatened, and therefore to bond with each other.

All these common values are symbolized by the American flag, which flies everywhere across the country, planted in every conceivable, possible, and even impossible place: front lawns, car windows, the sides of buildings, corporate websites. Its ideology is materialized through the common lifestyle that keeps the US coherent as a nation, the proliferation of monopoly capitalism that makes most American cities very similar to all others: not just the ubiquitous McDonalds, which has spread around the world, but Wallmart, JC Penney, Rich's, Chick-fil-A, Dunkin' Donuts, IHOP, Friendly's, Staples, Office-Max, and so on. You always know where you are when you are on the road in the US. The uniformity of American life is such that since the 1960s it has been able to allow the expression of minorities who proclaim the 'difference' of their identities; albeit permitted to the extent that anyone who lives in the US has to become absorbed in the relentless conformity of becoming 'American'. There is one significant kind of difference in the US, however, and that is an economic one: there are a lot of rich people in the US, but also a lot of poor people, many, many more poor people in fact. Hanging on to cultural differences masks over the cracks and successfully naturalizes the fact that some groups are rich, and other groups are poor.

And yet, this homogenizing approach to national identity has been very successful in the US. It does permit certain kinds of difference. The mistake of the postcolonial state was often that it took the alternative German Romantic account of the nation, developed at state level in Europe by Nazi Germany, as the only possible way in which a nation could be constructed: a holistic people with a common language, history, culture, and race. Though this model worked well for constructing a sense of solidarity and a goal for which people were fighting in the anti-colonial movements, the attempt to stabilize it and impose it by means of state control after independence has in general had disastrous consequences. Nationalism is Janus-faced: before independence, good; after independence, bad. This ambivalence means that postcolonialism itself can be appropriated in the name of a variety of contemporary cultural nationalisms, despite its theoretical orientation against them.

The Hindutva movement in India, with its ideology of a return to the authenticity of the golden age, of the wonder that was India, and its inalienable attachment to land that is peopled by minorities who wish to be independent (India administered Kashmir, obviously, but also those 'restricted areas' excepted in all foreigners' tourist visas, all along the northeastern frontier), has been the most recent national movement to pursue the illusions of national homogeneity derived from 19th-century Germanic ideas of authenticity. If you doubt the link, ask why newly printed copies of Hitler's *Mein Kampf* can be found for sale on street bookstalls all over northern India and Maharashtra. The project is the quest for authentic Indian-ness, for a *Hindu Rasthra*, an ethnically pure Hindu nation, which will eliminate or exclude minorities such as Muslims or Christians, and fix Dalits (untouchables) and Adivasis (tribals) into its eternal racial hierarchy of caste. The Hindutva movement mimics the history of its neighbour Sri Lanka, still caught in the grip of a frozen civil war that erupted after the homogenizing, but in practice exclusionary, 'Sinhala only' movement that was initiated against the Tamil minority after S. W. R. D. Bandaranaike's massive general election victory in 1956. People in the west always automatically assume that the western system of democracy must be the best political system for all countries of the world. However, in countries with well-defined, different ethnic groups, where one is in the large majority, democracy can become a form of popularly, democratically agreed tyranny and oppression. In such countries, the minority have no legitimate political means of resistance against the tyranny of the majority. Make your own list.

These repressive nationalist projects are not necessarily generated internally, however: nationalism, as Benedict Anderson has suggested, is often the creation of those who have left the country, and who, in safe and prosperous exile, fondly fund at long distance future recreations of idealized memories of their past. Is it the diasporic spread of a people beyond its borders that creates the nation? These nostalgic cultural imaginings are an effect of globalization, produced from afar by those who now never have to encounter the nation's everyday realities. According to an extensively documented report published in 2002, the explosive growth of Hindutva in India, which has under-girded much of the sectarian communal violence of the last decades, has been amply funded by a US charity, the India Development and Relief Fund, based in Maryland, despite US laws prohibiting such charities from engaging in political activities. Money from non-resident Indians in the US creates the link between the idealized past and its violent production by state governments and non-governmental organizations in the present. The racism and intolerance to which such holistic conceptions of the nation inevitably lead means that postcolonial intellectuals, particularly from India, have tried to think of the nation differently, to propose alternative accounts of the nation which begin not with an idealized version of how it might be, but with how it is, highlighting the ways in which the nation can work as a force of oppression. This means thinking of the postcolonial, or the postimperial, nation in terms of its fragments, those parts and those peoples who do not easily belong to it, who exist at the margins and peripheries of society. They are the means through which the nation relates to itself.

The ideal of the nation is often imaged as a woman, and the ideology of nationalism often invests the nation's core identity upon an idealized, patriarchal image of ideal womanhood. When this happens, women, as Virginia Woolf put it, effectively have no nation. Woman, refugee, asylum seeker . . . Throughout the 20th century, women have striven to resist patriarchal nationalism by forming transnational organizations. The uprising that was to topple the Russian Czar in 1917 began with demonstrations on International Women's Day. The great suffragette Sylvia Pankhurst affiliated to the First International Working Women's Congress held in Moscow in 1920. If many international women's and trade union movements during the first half of the 20th century were organized within the framework of the Soviet Comintern, in later decades the growth of women's movements was spearheaded by the United Nations Decade for Women between 1975 and 1985. Many transnational women's movements were then developed within the framework of the UN, of which the International Alliance of Women (IAW) has been the most prominent. Many others have grown independently, for example Development Alternatives with Women for a New Era (DAWN), which has branches in Latin America, the Caribbean, and Asia; the Women Living Under Muslim Laws International Solidarity Network (WLUML); or the Association of Women of the Mediterranean Region (AWMR), whose members come largely from North Africa and the eastern Mediterranean. Transnational movements and transnational links between resistance movements have been the most effective response to patriarchal national imperialisms throughout the century.

Resistance to the oppression of the colony or the nation can best be broken by cutting through its boundaries and reaching out beyond them.

While some nations try to sweep away their fragments, others are invented out of fragments: Indonesia, for example, was created by the Dutch, the Japanese, and the Javanese from uncontainable diversity that still threatens to tear it apart. Other nations live and die every day as fragments: take Palestine. The map of Palestine

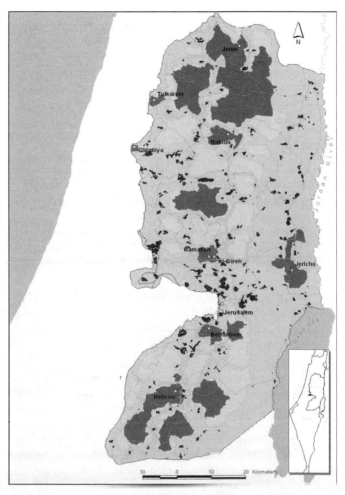

10. 'Palestine Bantustan': Map of the West Bank after the Oslo
Agreement.

after the Oslo Agreement looks like the night sky on a cloudy night. Whereas the stars have space between them, and the thousands of Indonesian islands have sea, Palestine has military checkpoints and Israeli-controlled territory in between its stars on its map.

Could these fragmented bits and pieces that make up the Occupied Territories ever seriously comprise a nation, a state, a homeland? This map vividly recalls other maps of an earlier colonial regime: the Bantustans, the tiny so-called independent homelands allocated to black South Africans during the apartheid era .

The wall

Most nations rely on cohesive borders. If borders are open, permeable, then the nation's peoples cannot be controlled. They may leave, others may enter illicitly: migrants, immigrants, undesirables. The modern state functions by means of a contradiction: a combination of strict border controls together with tolerance, even quiet encouragement, of illegal immigration – by workers who then have no rights.

So, make a boundary, build a wall. We are always surrounded by walls. The walls behind which people live have doors, entrances to go in and out, windows to see in and out, to open for fresh air and the stroke of the warm summer breeze.

Some of us are walled in. Walls around the cantonment, the prison compounds. 'Gated living' in the US, or South Africa: barricades.

Some of us are walled out. Many walls are no home. These are the ones with no windows. They are the walls that stretch through the countryside or zigzag across the city, built as border fences to keep people and things out. The limits of liberalism. To defend the state.

The virtual wall. Vietnam. 'The Virtual Wall™'. 'The faces of freedom™'. 'Clicking a photo on these indexes will display that person's complete memorial page.' Looking at their bright faces, reading the messages of their families, brings home so painfully the costs of trying to defend the state by encircling the earth. Not for the first time. The Great Wall of China, built to keep the Mongols out. Hadrian's Wall, built by the Romans to keep out the Picts. The Great Hedge of India, grown from Leia in the Punjab to the south of Burhanpur on the Maharashtran border to enforce the British Salt Tax that was eventually to be destroyed so effectively by Gandhi's Dandhi March in 1930. The rabbit-proof fence in Australia, built to keep rabbits from migrating and the stolen children of aboriginals from returning home across the countryside. The Berlin Wall, built to keep people in, in the anomaly of a divided city. The walls and fences now being built in the West Bank, across the middle of Palestinian farms, to keep the illegal Israeli settlers from the hostile Palestinians.

Border cities, especially those at the pressure points of direct contact between the first and third worlds: Ceuta and Melilla, the two Spanish colonies on the North African mainland. Like Martinique in the Caribbean, they are part of the European Union. With funds from Brussels, the two cities are surrounded by a ten-foot-high fence, with double razor-wire, electronic sensors, and infra-red cameras on top. Still the migrants, from Morocco, Algeria, and especially West Africa, try to climb in. Many of them are unaccompanied children. If caught, the Spanish authorities keep the children in residential centres, where they are often abused, and then illegally returned to Morocco, where they are then often beaten and abused again as a punishment by the Moroccan police, before being abandoned on unfamiliar streets late at night. Rather than risk being entangled in the razor-wire of the fence, many others pay large sums of money to risk a journey on rickety boats known as *pateras* to sail the nine-mile stretch across the treacherous waters to Spain. No one knows how many drown – somewhere between 1,000 and 2,000 people a year perhaps. Under pressure from the EU, the Spanish government has now installed a $120 million radar system that forms an electronic wall across the straits of Gibraltar. The migrants resort to taking more dangerous, longer routes across the water.

Tijuana, Mexico, is a city that has founded its relative prosperity on being a border town. The long street lines of the Avenida Revoluccion could be anywhere in the US. Only the colours give it away: compared to the pastels of California, they are wildly out of control. At the main intersection, the yellow and red of the Sara store faces the sky blue of the Lobster Club, which looks on to the bright purple of the 'Bar, Grill, Dance', opposite the pink and red of Le Drug Store. Any language but Spanish for this border town, a town turned inside out. Outside the city, late at night, young men, prospective migrants, gather by the River Levy. Operation Gatekeeper has been successful at keeping them out, its closed door producing what is called the Bonzai Run. Migrants run head-on into the traffic on Interstate 5 to avoid border control – it is simply so dangerous that the guards will not chase them. Or they swim the Rio Grande to be picked up and roughed up at gunpoint by local vigilante patrols in Eagle Pass, Texas. These are people slipping across into a land that was once theirs, from which they are now excluded. The busiest section of the border is called Imperial Beach.

Touch of Evil: cars parked at right angles all the way down the long stretch of the main street. Famously the film opens with an audacious crane-tracking shot that lasts three minutes as the camera works its way down four blocks of flashing neon lights interspersed with crumbling darkness towards the Mexican/US border, producing a seamlessness, a cinema without breaks, people without borders, borderless infiltration. A large convertible car driven by a wealthy American man and his blonde companion drives through the barrier checkpoint into the US. A moment later, the car explodes.

Chapter 4
Hybridity

Raï and Islamic social space

Much of this book has been inspired by, and the course of its writing frequently ripped apart by, the pulsating, energizing sounds of Algerian raï. Ideally, the book should also be read against the hoarse, pining pounding of 'Chabrassi', 'Guendozi Mama', or 'Wahlaich', the songs of Cheb Khaled, Cheikha Remitti, and Haïm. After the appalling experiences of the Algerian War of Independence – the widespread torture of men, women, and children; the million and a half Algerians killed by the French in their desperate attempt to retain their own privileges, won by imperial military conquest in the 19th century; the arbitrary occupation of a land whose people were never subdued – the emergence of raï music in the 1970s in Algeria was a particularly heartening phenomenon. Raï is often described as raw, rough, earthy (*trab*): it is also defiant, assertive, passionate. The singers throw themselves at its rhythms with an unimaginable fury that gives raï its unique energizing passion.

Raï began during the explosive population growth of the first generation of Algerians born after the end of the Algerian War of Independence in 1962. It came into its own in the late 1970s when singers from that generation, such as Sahraoui and Fadela, and Cheb Khaled, began to produce their own dynamic form of raï at

> It's something very powerful that I can't really explain. When I'm on stage, I don't cheat. I give everything I have in my soul and my spirit.
>
> **Cheikha Remitti, 2000**

once closer to western rock and reminiscent in its haunting self-expression of reggae and African-American blues. The emergence of raï is also associated with the migration of people throughout Algeria to the cities, and in that sense marks a syncretic musical form that epitomizes the economic imperatives of modernity. This involved much more than a process of fusion, synthesis, or intermixture. People and cultures do not flow unimpeded and unchanged in the way that capital does. The social production of raï was not a single process at all in fact, but rather involved histories of contested relations at every level of its production and consumption in Algerian society. To that extent raï can work too as a broader metaphor for thinking about the complex relations of cultures to the forces of modernity.

In the first place, raï does not consist of one kind of music that can easily be described in general terms. It has always been mobile and shifting as it changes its functions and locations, its instruments and its audiences. Its production is often casual and can be adapted easily according to specific needs. Its impromptu nature means that it will never become fixed, that it will always be flexible and able to incorporate new elements. At one level, it entails a spontaneous modernization (according to some, inevitably, a degeneration) of the traditional Arabic Maghrebian form of the *malhūn*, a traditional elaborate form of sung poetry performed by the *shīkhs*, learned, cultured religious men accorded high status for their art. In many ways, however, raï is more directly derived from the profane songs of the more transgressive and vibrant woman singers, the *shīkhas* who catered to the masculine spaces of the public bars and brothels of pre-Independence Algeria, performing also at weddings,

70

parties, and even religious festivals. The great Cheikha Remitti, generally accorded the title 'The Queen of Raï', began as, and in spirit has always remained, a *shīkha*, as her title suggests. Some women raï singers, on the other hand, started out as *maddāhas*, women poets who sing both religious and profane songs at gatherings exclusively for women at events such as circumcisions or *mendhis* prior to weddings.

As a musical form, raï originally developed soon after independence in the cosmopolitan port city of Wahrān (Oran), in western Algeria, where, particularly from the mid-1970s onwards, the young *chebs* (male singers such as Cheikh Meftah and Cheikh Djelloul Remchaoui) or *chabas* (women singers), singing in cabarets or at weddings, created new songs marked by radically honest lyrics about their own contemporary political and cultural situations. The titles *cheb/chab* that the performers were given, or gave themselves, marked their difference from traditional singers, suggesting their youthful audience, their lower social and artistic status, as well as signalling their innovative modern musical style. Musically, raï was in part adapted from the songs sung by the *shīkhs* in the *badawi*, or traditional Bedouin tradition, and in part from the more modern *wahrāni* music already developed in the cities since the 1930s from the *malhūn* and *andalus*, the classical city music of North Africa. *Wahrāni* music had already begun the process of transforming traditional Arabic musical forms to the demands of modern mass-produced music and electric instruments, beginning with the accordion, absorbing influences from Moroccan (*chaabi*) and Egyptian (especially Umm Kulthum, *Kawkab al-Sharq*, the Star of the Orient) dance and wedding music. This was now combined with elements of western rock, disco, and jazz, and West African music, together with songs from further afield such as Latin America and Bollywood – a range of sources that has no formal limits.

Raï performers originally began by using distinctive local acoustic instruments – string instruments such as the *'uud* (the Arabic lute); wind instruments such as the *gaṣba* and *nāy*, throaty haunting reed

71

flutes; percussion instruments such as the *banndīr* (tambourine), *gallāl* (drone), *qarqabu* (castanet), *darbūka*, *ṭbal*, and *ṭbila* (drums); together with the violin, accordion, and trumpet. From the earliest days, however, some musicians, such as the Qada and the Baba brothers, adapted their material for western electronic instruments and created 'electric' raï. In a similar way in linguistic terms, raï is sung in the local dialect, but a dialect inflected with running allusions and streetwise borrowings from Spanish, French, and Arabic. The development of raï was also precipitated by technological change: in some respects, it rose in its modern form in response to the specific demands of the local cassette-recording industry after the end of the vinyl record. The invention of cassettes for the first time put local entrepreneurs in control of music production, and much of raï's international success is owed to the producers and middlemen in Algeria and then France who have imposed their own needs and preferences in the recording studio on to the musical forms. It was never an 'authentic' music outside these motors of production; it developed through being played increasingly on radio stations abroad, primarily in Morocco and France. Although these commercialized conditions have been criticized in Algeria, at the same time this new situation allowed the music to emerge as an independent form and force, breaking established conventions within the musical and social culture of Algeria. It has always been, literally and metaphorically, multi-track.

The term 'raï' literally means 'an opinion', 'a point of view', 'a way of seeing things'; it can also mean 'an aim'. In terms of asserting its own perspectives, its own subversive will-to-power, therefore, raï encapsulates many of the qualities that are fundamental to postcolonialism itself. Beginning as the expression of those who found themselves on the periphery of their societies, immigrants to the cities who lived in deprived conditions of poverty, poor housing, and unemployment, raï's musical culture was quickly transformed out of the margins into the major popular expression for young people of social conditions within Algerian society. The speed with which raï spread in popularity across Algeria and North Africa was testimony to the degree to which it provided points of recognition that had never previously been articulated. It was quickly identified with 'the word of the people' (*shaab*), and to that degree became fundamentally articulated with the political message of the radical Islamist party *Front Islamique du Salut* (FIS). Raï's popular appeal lay in its recompositions of recognizable but destructured elements from the perspective of those at the margins through mass-produced popular modes. Raï singers took elements from a wide range of existent cultural forms – sacred, secular, classical, popular – and represented them in ways that took them out of their conventional contexts into new kinds of cultural expression. In invoking a range of complex cultural codes in forms that allowed spontaneous invention and elaboration, raï singers were able to express their own relations of contradiction and ambivalence towards the society around them, which was at once rapidly changing in economic terms and caught within rigid social structures. Raï stands in the contested space between modern interpretations of what constitute traditional Muslim values, and the traditional responses of accommodation and resistance to forces of historical change by Muslim societies.

These raï did not necessarily offer a way forward that had been thought through in political or ideological terms. Rather, they represented the emotional expression of those who found themselves at the points of disruption within Algerian society and on the wrong side of its forms of legitimation. Raï's popularity can be seen as a mark of its success in providing forms of identification to which many could immediately respond, particularly the *hittistes* ('those who prop up the wall'), whose primary adult experience was one of unemployment, boredom, and disillusion with the government. In political terms, raï, like many postcolonial cultural forms, was first of all concerned to articulate problems and situations, as a necessary first stage in moving towards any possible resolutions.

> I divide my career into three periods: the period of 78 records, the period of 45s, and the period of cassettes. Throughout all these periods, I have always sung the ordinary problems of life, social problems, yes, rebellion. The problems I saw were common problems, ever since the age of fifteen or sixteen. I still haven't got it all out. It's a matter of observing and reflecting. Raï music has always been a music of rebellion, a music that looks ahead.
>
> **Cheikha Remitti, 2000**

A hybrid genre of this kind says something about contemporary social problems, social contradictions: its politics are in its articulations, even its articulations of inarticulate states of being – it has no quick solutions, and may well have no immediate solutions at all. Like postcolonialism itself, it offers challenge rather than solution in the first instance, and allows its audiences themselves to interpret its new spaces with relevant meanings of their own. It does not arrive delivering its meaning already fully-formed – rather it enables new meanings to be created and projected in dialogic encounters. And like postcolonialism, because it articulates the raw, the rough, the vulgar, social and sexual tensions in a changing, torn social milieu that no longer adds up to a coherent civil society, it is criticized for its lack of respectability, for the impurity of its politics – as well as, in the case of raï, for the profanity of its language. For this reason, raï is also credited, or criticized, for its disruptive, destabilizing effects on its listeners as well as its performers – in other words, for producing the very effects that it names.

Rrāy l-ghaddār talaftli rrāy w khalītli d-dār

(Treacherous raï, you made me change my ways; you made me lose my home)

Cheb Khaled, 'Ntı, nti'

Clearly what raï does do is encourage forms of self-expression and identification in ways that in musical terms replicate some of the social tensions that it enunciates, particularly in the subversive borrowings from the traditional *shīkhs* set against electric sounds taken from commercial western rock, which express ambivalence between traditional cultural forms and aspirations towards the west. For at the same time, it continues to refuse the west by maintaining the distinctive Arabic fluid tonal sounds and rhythms: whereas western music, for example, is restricted by its notation system to half tones, Arabic music does not limit itself to set intervals, and freely moves amongst quarter and eighth tones. Its rhythms flow in an equally inventive pattern against the beat – only jazz since the 1950s comes remotely close to the musical inventiveness of Arabic music. In both cases, it is the extempore creativity of the performing musician that calls the music into being. In the same way, the singer's lyrics will forge traditional lines and refrains with references that incorporate the particular social world of his or her audience. By articulating within the songs recognizable local topics and cryptic allusions to places of transgressive love, such as the forest, as well as to the family and the sacred, raï forges a medium that speaks specifically to everyday forms and difficulties of Maghrebian experience, while itself being given meanings within the contexts of contemporary social life. The meanings are enacted through the performance. Raï does not represent either a search for, or a creation of, a new cultural identity. It is rather part of a process in which novel kinds of perceptions relating to cultural identity are staged, debated, and negotiated in challenging ways that were not previously possible.

At independence in 1962 the initial position of the state towards Algerian music was to patronize the traditional culture of *andalus*, the national classical music enjoyed primarily by the Algerian elite, and to dismiss the raï that was exploding from the streets in its synthesis of traditional and modern popular forms. From the mid-1980s, however, as raï rose to international prominence, government attitudes changed dramatically, and raï began to be patronized by official channels of the state, with raï concerts promoted by the ruling FLN elite. At this point, the identity of raï as the word of the people began to be contested more actively by Islamists, and it was denounced by the FIS as morally decadent. After one of raï's most famous singers, Cheb Hasni, was assassinated in October 1994, many others have sought refuge, ironically, in France. Despite the civil war that began in 1988 and the increasing dominance of the Islamist party, raï remains the dominant popular musical form amongst young Algerians, and continues to mediate their interests in the west with their strong attraction to Islamism.

From the mid-1980s raï was also promoted within France, and achieved a wide following across the Maghreb as well as in North African communities in France, Spain, and elsewhere. It was one of the first examples of so-called 'world music'. This concept, which emerged in the late 1980s, is often described in terms of 'fusion': a fusion of western elements, of rock and jazz, with the tonal harmonics, rhythms, and particular sounds of local music. Fusion marks a phenomenon of globalization in which the cultural channels of communication have been opened for all by technology, which intersects different musical sounds with ease – quite literally, in fact, on the synthesizer. In some cases, the simple idea that these elements have fused together into new mixed modes may well be accurate, though it is notable that some raï songs, such as Haïm's 'Wahlaich', were simultaneously produced in Arab and French versions. It is also striking that apparently homogenizing tendencies can lead to very specific local forms. The sound of Raïna Raï, who come from Algiers, for example, is distinctly different from the traditional earthy or popular forms of raï that first emerged along the Wahrān coastline.

In contrast to its varied and ambivalent role in Algerian society, in its presentation to the west, raï has been brought in to tell a familiar story – the story that the west always wants to hear about other cultures that appear to operate according to norms significantly different to its own, and which resist accommodation and incorporation into western economic and ideological models. As reported in the French and world press, raï has been turned into a western-style Algerian youth revolt, and presented as a second, postcolonial war of liberation and modernity against paternalist tradition, a revolution against the social rigidities and disparities of wealth under the current Algerian regime, and as a secularist revolt by Algerian youth against the strictures of Islamism in Algeria, above all breaking through social and religious taboos on sexuality, alcohol, and drugs. Raï singers have been profiled as bohemian rebels who aspire to express a free individualism that emulates the commercial individualism of the west and allies them to international pop icons of rebellion such as James Dean, to punk, rap, and reggae. As the sleeve of a raï anthology puts it:

> Raï stars . . . love to state what time it is. Not that they like to waste words on religious or political issues – rising from the town of Oran in west Algerian in the '80s, raï was a celebration of good times in a place where good times were desperately hard to find. Sex 'n' drugs 'n' raï 'n' roll. Right on said Algeria's disaffected youth massive. Ruled out said Algeria's fundamentalist Islamic Front and military government, united in a hatred of raï's striving for freedom.

Here raï has been accommodated to the strict protocols of western youth culture – whose demands would not tolerate stories of its active promotion by the Algerian government, for example. In the versions produced for the French and British record labels, moreover, the music itself has been adapted to suit western tastes. In Khaled's songs, recorded with American musicians in Los Angeles for the 1992 album *Khaled* (the transition to the west was formally marked by his dropping the title Cheb), the distinctive and infinitely flexible three-beat rhythm of raï (triplets, in which the singer often freely extemporizes after the first beat) has been replaced by the mechanical fixed four-beat rhythm of western disco, with the addition of a recognizable western-style harmonized chorus. Khaled's voice, meanwhile, seems to refuse all smoothed-out fusion, rasping out its Arabic on a separate track far off in its own orbit, living altogether in another spatial rhythm and temporality. The commercial processes have also been westernized: whereas raï songs in Algeria were produced spontaneously from a shifting range of communal sources, freely adaptable by all, Khaled's record company have registered him with the copyright authorities in France as the writer of all the songs he had previously recorded in Algeria, even when they were old songs of Cheikha Remitti and others that in Algeria had never been regarded as anyone's private property. It is unlikely, of course, that raï would ever have become popular in the west without some modifications, any more than western music gets appropriated straight in the Maghreb. Moreover, as has been suggested, raï is itself a complex, changing musical form that remains adaptable and flexible: 'French' raï by Johanne Hayat or Malik is also popular in Algeria, while Algerian singers increasingly sing only *rrāy nqī* (clean raï) – with all its Islamic implications of propriety. At the same time, raï in the west was not just designed for consumption by the regular western pop market: it was always driven by diasporic North African communities in France, Britain, and North America who demanded none of the requirements of western conventions.

The CD cover picture in Figure 11 conveys some important elements of raï rather better than its sleeve notes: its vibrancy and energy, its relations to masculinity, to the everyday experience of young Algerians on the streets, its continued active and positive relations to Islam, here signalled in the prominent prayer *Bismillāh-ir-Rahmānir Rahīm* (in the name of Allah, the gracious, the merciful), that closes and supports the whole image in the lower right corner. The montage thus gives something of a visual equivalent of raï's mixed social and religious identity. Raï has often been described as 'hybrid'. In fact, it encapsulates many of the qualities that the term 'hybridity' in postcolonial writing attempts to locate. Like raï, hybridity does not involve a single process, though it can sometimes be discussed in unimaginative abstract terms far from any consideration of the dynamic dimensions of cultural formation and

11. Cover of raï compilation CD, Manteca World Music, 2000.

contestation such as to be found in raï. Hybridity works in different ways at the same time, according to the cultural, economic, and political demands of specific situations. It involves processes of interaction that create new social spaces to which new meanings are given. These relations enable the articulation of experiences of change in societies splintered by modernity, and they facilitate consequent demands for social transformation. So it is with raï. As a hybrid popular form, often working in complex and sometimes covert ways by allusion and inference, raï has offered a creative space of articulation and demand, revolt and resistance, innovation and negotiation, for many of the contradictory social and economic channels operating and developing within contemporary Algerian society.

The ambivalence of the veil

Nothing symbolizes the differences between the western and the Muslim worlds more than the veil. Few items of clothing throughout history can have been given more meanings and political significances. For Europeans, the veil used to symbolize the erotic mysteries of the east. For Muslims, it signified social status. Today, the meaning of the veil has changed dramatically. For many westerners, the veil is a symbol of patriarchal Islamic societies in which women are assumed to be oppressed, subordinated, and made invisible. On the other hand, in Islamic societies, and among many Muslim women in non-Islamic societies, the veil (*hijab*) has come to symbolize a cultural and religious identity, and women have increasingly chosen to cover themselves as a matter of choice. As a result, the veil is more widely worn today than ever before. Today, depending who you are, the veil symbolizes control or defiance, oppression or autonomy, patriarchy or non-western communal values. How can we understand the veil, catch its meanings, and at the same time take hold of and interrogate our own automated responses? No one can read the veil from a neutral, disinterested space. Let us try by first looking at an image (Figure 12) that typifies the kind of European stereotypical representations of the east in the colonial period, of the kind characterized by Edward Said as 'Orientalism'.

The image is entitled simply 'Arab woman'. A colour postcard, dating from around 1910, the high noon of imperialism, it was produced in Egypt by one of the many German photographic firms based in the Middle East at that time. The representation has objectified the woman it depicts. A real Egyptian woman, with a name, a family, a voice, and a history, has been transformed into an 'Oriental', a universal, generic 'Arab Woman'. The woman has been specially constructed for the eye of power suspended in the westerner's gaze, and precipitated into the one-way street of 'the politics of recognition'.

12. 'Arab woman'.

Is this a photograph or a painting? She wears a brown veil, with a yellow lining that falls over her shoulders and a cloth of bluish-green. A *burqa* of black wrinkled cotton, held up by a *basma*, a piece of cloth that runs through the protruding *'oqla*, made from a piece of a special kind of bamboo called *Farsi*, covers the lower part of her face, but leaves much of her forehead and upper cheekbones exposed. She is looking away from the camera, thus increasing her modesty while at the same time giving her a thoughtful, distracted look. Looking at the coarse bluish cloth of her *galabiya* that falls in folds over the rest of her body, it seems that the artist has subliminally cast her in the pose of the Virgin Mary. A Virgin Mary, decently veiled, as no doubt she was, and it might seem predominantly passive, receptive. All she lacks is the halo, but the aura of quietude around this woman is so strong that she hardly needs one. With her averted gaze, and her arms lowered and folded around her body, it is as if she could never speak, or act, for herself.

Or is it we as viewers who assume this? Does this representation of a woman give us what the artist wanted us to see, a certain image of 'the Arab woman', an exotic oriental woman who can stand for all Arab women, as opposed to the reality of what this particular woman was really like? The image never asks us to think of her as a living human being in a social environment. It is constructed for a certain kind of western viewer who already knows from many other representations what an 'Arab woman' ought to look like – modest, pining, above all veiled. The European knows her instantly, just as today we recognize a picture of a cosy snow-covered scene as an image of Christmas. A representation of Christmas has to show us a snow-covered scene if it is going to evoke Christmas properly. This is the case even though in many, if not most, places of the world, Christmas actually never looks like that. In England, for example, it is generally a mild day with a bit of sunshine and drizzle. There is very rarely any snow. To show a drizzly day on a card, however, would not evoke 'Christmas' in the way a snow-scene does – even when we know that, in terms of our experience, the mythical White Christmas is completely untrue.

> What does need to be questioned, however, is the *mode of representation of otherness.*
>
> Homi K. Bhabha, *The Location of Culture* (1994)

So too with this woman. Though her veiling here is not as extreme as in the full *burqa*, the tubular *'oqla* sticking out so prominently on the forehead, and the tightly drawn long black cloth round the cheekbones over the mouth, narrowing as it descends towards the waist like an enormous beak, give a strong impression to western eyes of imprisonment. She seems literally confined, caged, exhibiting every quality that many western women and men have considered that Muslim women need freeing from by the enlightened, unveiled west – the undressed west, which demands that women uncover themselves, whether they want to or not. In the 19th century, the west considered the wearing of clothes as the mark of civilization; it was 'savages' who went naked. In the 20th and 21st centuries, however, semi-nudity became the signifier of western superiority.

The two layers of colour of the chromolithograph have not been swept over her eyes, leaving them almost matt, so that if you look closely at the pupils they are printed in black and white, staring out from behind the colours that veil her. You begin to see that her eyes are resourceful, strong, empowered, despite the aesthetic frame that has been put around her – which is far more repressive of what she really is than any veil could ever be. The stereotypical image becomes increasingly difficult to read. The woman who has been objectified seems to turn the tables and reassert herself against the power of the western gaze.

In the course of the 20th century, the veil increasingly became a focus for those who sought to secularize Islamic societies. The French in Algeria and elsewhere initiated the 'Battle of the Veil', carrying out forced unveilings of local women. As part of his attempt to westernize Iran, the western-imposed Shah of Iran banned the *chador*, the black head-to-toe body wrap worn by rural and traditional urban women. In direct response, after the Islamic Revolution of 1978/79, women were required to wear it. If some women can be considered to be persecuted by being forced to wear the veil, as westerners generally assume, then other women are equally persecuted by secular laws that oblige them not to wear it. In France and Spain, for example, girls have to fight in the courts to go to school with their heads covered. Here, we are not talking about a veil like the one the Egyptian woman is wearing, where a few curls on the forehead are allowed to break the severity of the veil's boundary, but a veil that completely covers the hair (just as, until fairly recently, European Catholic women used to wear a mantle over their heads when going to church). In Turkey, the enlightened legislation of a secular state in a Muslim country at present prohibits the wearing of any kind of veil in public institutions such as schools, universities, and even hospitals. As a result, many women who have chosen to dress as 'covered women' are prevented from going to university at all. Ways round it can, of course, always be found. One woman, who is a doctor, appropriates an old Jewish custom for married women, and obeys the letter of the law by always wearing a wig, thus revealing hair but at the same time keeping her own hair hidden and out of sight. In the most recent Turkish election, an Islamic party gained power that promised finally to reverse this law that drives Turkish women to study in universities in Berlin, London, and Vienna (in Turkey, they joke that this second Siege of Vienna has been more successful than the first). Men can attend university in Turkey because there is no parallel law demanding that all male university students be hatless and clean-shaven so as to reveal all of their heads and faces. Having said that, it remains the case that Kemal Attaturk, the founder of modern Turkey, did ban the *fez*, and historically much of the legislation about dress in Turkey and Iran was focused on male dress.

84

When people talk about 'the veil', they often end up talking about it as if it were a fixed thing, like a piece of uniform. There is not just 'the veil' – there are many kinds of veil, and in most societies at any given moment different women will be wearing a great variety of them, in untroubled heterogeneity. The veil itself is a fluid, ambivalent garment. There are the body veils, the *abaya*, the *burqa*, the *chador*, the *chadri*, the *carsaf* or *khimar*, the *haik*, and the *sitara*. Then there are the face or head veils, the *batula*, the *boushiya*, the *burko*, the *dupatta*, the *hijab*, the *niqaab*, the *rouband*, and the *yasmak*, to name only some of the most popular. While there are many different kinds of veil, and many different ways in which women wear any particular veil at different times, like any clothing, veils also change, shift, modify, and are adapted to different needs and new circumstances.

Such as colonial occupation, for example. Fanon emphasized the 'historic dynamism of the veil', the ways in which it can be changed strategically and used instrumentally according to circumstance. This was particularly apparent during the Algerian War of Independence, when the division between the *colons* (settlers) and the natives was such that a woman affiliated herself to either side according to her style of dress. As in the famous scenes in Pontecorvo's film *Battle of Algiers* (1965), Algerian women could then be sent as invisible couriers to carry weapons or plant bombs in the European parts of the city.

> The protective mantle of the Casbah, the almost organic curtain of safety that the Arab town weaves round the native, withdrew, and the Algerian woman, exposed, was sent forth into the conqueror's city.
>
> Frantz Fanon

By turns, Algeria veiled and unveiled itself, playing against the assumptions of the colonial occupier. Although the French soldiers were officially given leaflets telling them to respect Muslim women, there were plenty of other well-documented occasions when the demands of their investigative processes, *la torture*, resulted in the rape, torture, and killing of suspects. Sometimes these women were paraded bound and naked by their captors, and photographed in that state before their death. Algeria unveiled – for the cruel eyes of French 'civilization'.

'This woman who sees without being seen frustrates the colonizer', says Fanon. She asserts a resisting refusal of knowledge comparable only to the impenetrability of the Casbah, the fortress in whose steep, narrow alleyways the ambivalent veiled woman is often pictured. The nature of the western response to the veil is to demand and desire its removal, so that strategies of liberation in the name of saving women supposedly forced to wear the veil coincide uncomfortably with the colonial violence of the veil's forcible removal. Fanon himself had to learn that despite his emphasis on community in his psychiatric hospital at Blida in northern Algeria, he had to allow the creation of a separate section in the hospital canteen for women.

Is it veiling or unveiling that constitutes the radical assertive move against institutionalized forms of power? It is only recently, when it has been made clear that many women choose to wear the veil and will fight for the right to do so, that veiling has been associated with militancy amongst women. For men, by contrast, to wear the face veiled carries completely different connotations from those associated with the Arab woman. Take the photograph in Figure 13, for example, of Subcommandante Marcos of the Zapatistas riding triumphantly into Mexico City in 2001. Marcos has just criss-crossed the country in a 15-day march gathering support for his bill to increase rights of autonomy and land ownership for Mexico's still impoverished indigenous Indians. The government has finally agreed to negotiate with him, and Marcos rides into the city. It is a moment of popular frenzy. He is masked, garlanded, a popular hero. Notice, too, the homely, fatherly touch of the pipe, which emerges mysteriously from his hidden lips.

13. Subcommandante Marcos arriving in Mexico City, 10 March 2001.

To cover the face, for a man, carries all the connotations of wearing a masque – of romantic banditry, of being outlawed, adopting a disguise as a means of self-protection against the odds of the authority in power. The Zapatistas' war against the Mexican state on behalf of the indigenous peasantry of southern Mexico, who, despite rebellions throughout their history, have won few rights of land and property, has famously been one in which indigenous rights have been asserted through the most modern forms of technology. Marcos used to fax his demands to the government and the papers: now he sends them by email. At the same time, the Zapatistas have employed as their hallmark the balaclava helmet, a veil that, like the masks of the Intifada fighters in Palestine, both guards their identity from the security forces and gives them a militant uniform. The very uniformity that the veil appears to impose on the woman here increases the masculine subversive resonance. The male veil is assertive. Whereas the Arab woman keeps demurely still, the garlanded Marcos raises his open hand triumphantly high in the air, and though he too looks to the side of the camera, he is clearly saluting a crowd, not averting his eyes from the viewer. We, as onlookers, are reduced to being part of the spectacle of which he is the centre. Why does the veil appear to disempower a woman, but empower a man?

The answer is that this is not intrinsically a gender issue but a situational one. There are also examples of veiling of Arab men, such as among the Berber Hamitic-speaking Tuareg, who regard the veil as an instrument of social status and masculinity. Tuareg men wear a white or blue veil called the *tegelmoust*. The Egyptian-born anthropologist Fadwa El Guindi writes,

> The veil is worn continually by men – at home, travelling, during the evening or day, eating or smoking, sleeping and even, according to some sources, during sexual intercourse.

Tuareg women, on the other hand, are not face-veiled at all, though they use their shawls to cover the lower part of the face rather as older women in South Asia use the *dupatta*. What is striking about Tuareg male veiling is the way that it is also used as a mobile signifier to denote meanings in everyday ordinary social intercourse. The veil is drawn up to the eyes before women, strangers, or prestigious persons, lowered amongst those for whom the wearer feels less respect. Rather as with the *dhoti* in southern India, which men unconsciously adjust, fold, wrap, and hitch up to knee length, then unfold and drop, as they stand talking to each other, Tuareg men are continually adjusting and readjusting their veils, heightening and tightening them, lowering and slackening, tugging and straightening them, as they go about their daily business.

The veil, in other words, can only be read in terms of its local meanings, which are generated within its own social space. A reading from outside will always tend to impose meanings from the social space of the viewer. For westerners, the veil is about the subordination and oppression of women. In Arabic societies, as El Guindi comments, 'the veil is about privacy, identity, kinship status, rank and class'. Whereas the western viewer, therefore, typically sees the photograph of the veiled Arab woman as a symbol of women's oppression under Islam, for an Egyptian looking at her image in 1910, the veil would have symbolized the woman's social rank. Women of the lowest class, particularly the peasantry in the countryside and the bedouin women of the desert, would not have worn a veil at all. Within the cities, women of different classes wore different kinds of veil. Upper-class Egyptian women wore the Turkish-style *bisha*, made of white muslin. The woman in the postcard, by contrast, wears a traditional black face-veil and *'oqla*, which, together with her *galabiya*, suggests that she belongs to the lower classes of artisans, labourers, or market women. While to the western viewer, therefore, her image may suggest either biblical resonances or an oppressive patriarchal social system, to an Egyptian, her veil first and foremost would have defined her social status. The western viewer, in other words, with no local cultural knowledge, would give a completely different interpretation of the photograph to that of the contemporary Egyptian woman whom it represented.

Nowadays the veil involves a different kind of cultural power, particularly with respect to western societies. Take Figure 14, for example, in which the veiled black woman clearly communicates her challenge directly to the viewer. Her eyes are wide open, and she looks straight at the camera. Notice, too, how the image is taken close up, in an in-your-face way, rather than inviting the aesthetic distance through which we saw the Arab woman. Our response is mediated by the information provided by the title, which tells us that she is a Muslim woman photographed in Brooklyn, New York. The fact that she is in New York encourages the viewer to assume that she is an African-American woman who is probably a member of the Nation of Islam. She has chosen the veil, in the society in which it currently has the most confrontational meaning.

Veil, mask: compliance or defiance? And agency: who chooses to veil themselves? In fact, the women's and the Zapatistas' choice of veiling are responses to the society in which they live. It might seem that the Egyptian woman has no option within a patriarchal system but to veil herself, while Marcos has been a free agent who makes a choice. However, as we have seen, in fact in Egypt in the earlier part of the 20th century, veiling for a woman was generally a mark of status, and in that sense was therefore regarded as empowering rather than disempowering. One reason veiling became more widespread was because more and more women wanted to assert social status, particularly to other women.

For Marcos, as a revolutionary fighting his government, his anonymity is a strategic requirement. He chose to wear the balaclava, but not as an act of free choice. In modern times, covering the face has become a widespread means of avoiding identification by police cameras, a device always used, for example, at IRA funerals. It also represents an act of defiance and assertion, as veiling increasingly does for Islamic women today. The meaning of

14. 'Muslim woman in Brooklyn' by Chester Higgins Jr.

the veil, when it has one, is never stable. Fanon recalls how under colonial rule Moroccan women changed the colour of their veil from white to black to express solidarity with their exiled king: they chose to give the veil a meaning by transforming its colour. More often, reading the veil amounts to how the veil looks out of its own social context, to what the exterior viewer puts into his or her interpretation, and has very little to do with what the veil means for the actual woman who is wearing it.

Chapter 5
Postcolonial feminism

Gendering politics in India

The women were furious with him when he left the ashram. It had all been so carefully planned. The route, the places they would eat, the places they would sleep, the beaches where they would finally break the law. Why did he refuse to allow any women to go with him? He who had done so much to put women at the centre of his politics, of his style of campaigning, of his very definition of what makes the political. He actively encouraged the political participation of women, identified with many feminist causes, and recognized the potential of feminist political strategies. He used to say that his politics were above all inspired by the tactics of the British suffragettes and Sinn Féin: moral rather than physical force. The violence only of the fast, the hunger strike, and the march. Gandhi was by no means the first to politicize the weapons of the weak, weapons that anyone could share.

Still, he absolutely refused to allow it, however much Sarojini Naidu and even Mira Behn remonstrated with him. The men set off that morning for the sea, in their starched *kurtas* and caps, all supplied with a long walking stick that the women had cut for them. The women were left behind once again, waiting for news, denied political agency once more. The whole world was watching, the film crews were at the ready. Not a woman would be seen. Yet it was he himself who, while in South Africa in 1913, had asked the Transvaal sisters to volunteer to sacrifice themselves at Phoenix Farm by undertaking a *satyagraha* that would lead them to run the risk of a jail sentence, which indeed they duly received, at the cost of the life of one of them, a 16-year-old girl from Johannesburg. The imprisoning of Indian women in South Africa, he noticed, 'stirred the hearts of the Indians not only in South Africa but also in the motherland to its very depths'. He saw how 'passive resistance', as Sri Aurobindo had originally called it, could work more effectively with women as its agents, and considered women most suited to *satyagraha* technique. The Civil Disobedience campaigns brought the participation of women to the centre of political activism; in the Bardoli campaign women such as Bhaktiba, Sharda Mehta, and Mithiben Petit were particularly prominent. It was he who identified not with the political urban elite, but with those at the margins, peasant men and women, the indigo workers in Bihar, as well as women more generally. By championing *khādī*, homegrown cloth, against cheap imported cotton from Lancashire, he initiated the whole means by which women and men could make a political statement simply through their dress (those who could afford it at least).

It was Gandhi who symbolized his entire political and cultural campaign by the act of spinning – a traditionally feminine activity, as the term 'spinster' suggests. He often even projected himself as a woman, and not just as an androgynous spinster:

> I knew, and so did the children, that I loved them with a mother's love ... My eye always followed the girls as a mother's eye would follow a daughter.

When their sexuality threatened to arouse the boys, however, his response was more that of the puritanical male:

> In the morning I gently suggested to the girls that they might let me cut off their fine long hair.

Gandhi was always very keen on giving things up, on renunciation – which was all very fine if you had had it in the first place. He preferred his feminine principle *shakti* ('soul power') to be androgynized, fearing women's sexuality, and so favoured the spinster and the sister ('behn') over the wife – which is indeed what he made his own wife become. Even while himself appropriating 'feminized' modes of struggle, Gandhi tended to project women in traditional roles. His ideas about sexuality and the domestic role of women in many ways simply reinforced traditional Hindu and puritanical Victorian concepts of women and femininity: Gandhi always promulgated traditional values such as Sita's loyalty to her husband. He was a reformer, but not as automatically sympathetic to progressive ideas about women's rights in the way Nehru was. But then Nehru came out of a communist tradition in which women's rights were an unquestioned part of the removal of all institutional structures of inequality.

All the same, Gandhi was prescient, and recognized that anti-colonial politics were of limited use without more radical social reform. He was no regular anti-colonial nationalist. Gandhi wanted to reform Indian society, its castism, its social and gender inequalities, as well as getting rid of the British. To that extent he anticipated many of the political strategies of postcolonial feminist activism, fighting for women's rights in a whole range of ways. His doctrine of non-violence was not just a strategy for dealing with the British: it also marked the basis for equitable relations between men and women, for a sustainable relationship to the environment, and a practice of diet and natural medicine that encouraged non-violent forms of intervention with respect to our own bodies. He was in that sense the first Green politician. He saw how women's politics were more radical than most nationalisms, how their denial of the divisions between public and private space transgressed the masculine political authority of the colonial regime.

Gender and modernity

At the same time, Gandhi's critique of modernity could be problematic for women, for whom the politics of modernity were more advantageous. Many characteristics of modernity, in fact, were themselves the invention of women. Modernity is defined by both by its technology and its political concepts of equality and democracy, which necessarily involve the end of patriarchy and the institution of equal rights for women. For many male nationalists, on the other hand, modernity was a matter of re-orienting the economy, the state, the public sphere. Even today, as the Indian novelist Arundhati Roy has acerbically pointed out, the Hindutva quest for authentic Indianness would not go so far as dispensing with the mobile phone, the railways, aeroplanes, or rockets that deliver atomic bombs. Gandhi was in fact much more radical than modern Hindutva ideologues in extending his critique of western civilization to science and technology, rejecting the railways and other aspects of colonial modernity in *Hind Swaraj* ('Indian Home Rule', published in 1909) His ideas were the forerunner of contemporary notions of 'sustainable development', the art of the possible.

When nationalism moved from reform movements to cultural revival, feminists began to part company from it, while continuing

> Thus, to simply denounce Third World women's oppression with notions and terms made to reflect or fit into Euro-American women's criteria of equality is to abide by ethnographic ideology ... which depends on the representation of a coherent cultural subject as source of scientific knowledge to explain a native culture and reduces every gendered activity to a sex-role stereotype. Feminism in such a context may well mean 'westernization'.
>
> Trin T. Minh-ha, *Woman, Native, Other* (1990)

to appropriate elements of modernity for their own political goals. Cultural nationalists tended to define themselves not against modernity in terms of technology, but against its implications for women. Women are often taken to represent the mainstay of the cultural identity of the nation, retrieved for the present from the society of the past. For macho-nationalists, home and the domestic sphere, relatively free from colonial control, was the best guardian of the traditional values, culture, and identity of the new phenomenon they were creating on the European model against their European masters, 'the nation'. Women and modernity came to be regarded as antithetical entities, with the result that the goal of national emancipation involved a betrayal of all prospect of progressive change for women. This was spectacularly dramatized in India and Africa on the occasions when the colonial government attempted to outlaw practices such as child marriage, widow-burning, and female genital mutilation. The preservation of these practices became celebrated causes for nationalist resistance (though not by Gandhi or Nehru).

These interventions by the colonial state against social practices that oppressed women have been described as 'colonial feminism', that is where the colonial government intervened on behalf of women, claiming it was doing so on humanitarian grounds. Sometimes these measures operated simultaneously as forms of colonial control. The colonial authorities were often sympathetic to those interventions that they regarded as a way of transforming the values of societies whose traditions resisted their rule. This was clearest with respect to the French colonial policy of forced unveiling in the Maghreb. In all cases, it was entirely predictable that such legislative acts would become the focus for nationalist resistance. Yet paradoxically, for women colonial ideology could represent new forms of freedom. As a result, women were much more ambivalently placed in relation both to colonialism and anti-colonial nationalism. This has also meant that while women struggle with the legacies of colonialism in the postcolonial era, they are repeatedly accused of importing western ideas. Well-meaning interventions by western feminists, human rights groups, and Ford Foundation-funded non-governmental organizations can at times end up by making life more complicated for local feminists. Development of all kinds comes best from below rather than being imposed from above.

At the same time, if you argue that feminism is a western idea then you would have to claim that modernity itself is exclusively western. Historically, it is true that feminism was a western political movement that began in the 18th century. Its beginnings were indistinguishable from those of modernity itself. Modernity, we would now argue, was not a western invention as such but itself a product of the west's interaction with the rest of the world, including the economic exploitation of colonialism which first provided the surplus gold that was the motor for modern capitalism. Since then modernity has developed in different ways and according to different temporalities in different places, and the same is true of feminism. Like other aspects of modernity, its development over the past two centuries within non-western worlds has transformed and nuanced its precepts. All political programmes of today, whether feminist or fundamentalist, are products of their own age and therefore very much part of modernity. The debate is not between modernity and its opponents, but rather between different versions of modernity, some of which offer alternatives to what is regarded, not always very accurately, as the western model.

Women's movements after independence

Many of these differences remained relatively suppressed while men and women worked together for the common aims of the anti-colonial movements. It was after independence that fundamental tensions emerged more clearly. 'The role of women does not end with peace' was the simple but astute title of an article by Amina al-Sa'id about Egyptian women volunteering for the army in 1956. For all feminists, the transfer of power at independence and the achievement of national sovereignty, though desirable, was not the

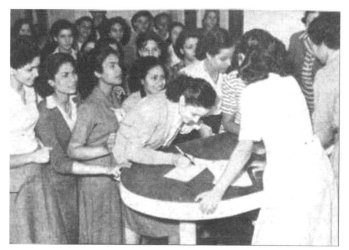

15. Egyptian women volunteer for popular resistance movements against British occupation.

end. It was simply a stage along the way. Whereas from a masculine perspective, independence ushered in the defining new condition of postcoloniality, for women there was no such break: the struggle continued, now against a patriarchal sphere that no longer required women's support. Independence very often involved a transfer of power not to the people of the newly sovereign country, but to local elites who inherited the whole colonial system of the army, the police, the judiciary and the law, government bureaucracy, and development agencies. In many states, after the bulk of energy had been dedicated to achieving national sovereignty, at independence women's political objectives had to be reasserted and a second liberation struggle begun. For this reason, postcolonial politics has often more in common with women's than men's struggles of the colonial era, with a politics of egalitarianism that supports diversity rather than the cultural uniformity demanded for nationalism.

The striking development of religious nationalisms in the postcolonial era – which in certain respects has even defined the postcolonial era – has actually placed women in a situation comparable to that in which they found themselves during colonialism. It is not, however, simply that women in Islamic countries are oppressed by fundamentalism or by Islam, as liberals in the west often assume. There is no single Islam, nor a single Islamic fundamentalism. Women in Islamic countries are positioned in relation to the specificities of their own cultures, their own histories, their own relations to the west and to western colonial power, their own struggles over the interpretation of Islam and of Islamic law, and their relation to the role of women in contemporary society.

Conversely, contrary to the violent polemics against it that can be found in many tricontinental countries around the globe, there is no single undifferentiated 'west' either. The fractures within the west were seen very clearly by Gandhi, and he exploited them actively for India's political advantage.

Feminism and ecology

Although Gandhi's influence has now waned dramatically in India, some elements of his political philosophy continue in a straightforward way. The Chipko movement in India, for example, which is largely organized by women, has been traced back directly by Vandana Shiva to beginnings initiated by Mira Behn, one of the women closest to Gandhi. Shiva has argued that national colonization brought with it a colonization of living natural resources such as the forests, and then a mental colonization in its prescription of technological and market-oriented responses to farming and environmental issues. Resistance by peasants and tribals to the appropriation of forests began in the colonial period, when timber was exploited for military and industrial purposes without thought to the longer-term effects of deforestation and desertification or for the consequence of the destruction of closely interrelated local economies and ecologies.

In the late 1940s, shortly before Gandhi's assassination, Mira Behn moved to a farm in the foothills of the Himalayas. There she became increasingly concerned with the devastating annual flooding that occurred in the region, the causes of which, as she discovered, were both deforestation and the planting of new kinds of non-indigenous trees, particularly pines. Mira Behn established a new ashram, Gopal Ashram, in order to concentrate on the forest problem. She studied the local environment and, particularly, spent time acquiring knowledge about it from the local people who knew it intimately. Listening to their songs and folktales, Mira Behn noticed the many references to trees and plants that had more or less disappeared. She concluded that the ecological problems experienced in the area were the result of the disappearance of the forests of oak (*banj*). Whereas oak contributed positively to the ecological environment and the local economy, the pine, which had been more recently planted for purely commercial reasons, was an evergreen that contributed nothing to the local ecological economy, providing only cash crops of resin and wood pulp. Soon other Gandhians such as Sarala Behn and Sunderlal Bahuguna joined Mira Behn in her work and established new ashrams.

As the movement grew, a significant division developed which was essentially a gendered one. Initially the focus of many local Gandhian organizations was on establishing cooperatives and asserting the rights of local people rather than big commercial firms to exploit the wood of the forest as a commercial cash crop. This, Shiva suggests, was essentially a masculist perspective. The women, who were responsible for cultivation of food crops and for fetching fuel and fodder, were not seduced by short-term advantages of

As usual, in every scheme that worsens the position of the poor, it is the poor who are invoked as beneficiaries.

Vandana Shiva

monocultural cash crops. They rather emphasized the need for a sustainable local ecology in which vegetation, soil, and water formed a complex interrelated ecosystem. The divisions, therefore, were not only between the outsiders and the locals, but between the women and the men of the villages. The women challenged the principles of the whole system, charging that the men had been ideologically colonized by the short-term commercial values of the market place, trying to take control of nature just as patriarchy tries to control women. The women's perspective was not driven by the prospect of immediate gain through employing science to dominate nature but by the objective of a supportive, self-renewing forest system that preserved water and food resources. Their long-standing role of being the cultivators, of producing sustenance enabling their families to survive within this system, meant that the women possessed repositories of intimate knowledge both of husbandry and of the medicinal and nutritional value of a wide variety of plants.

It was therefore the women, together with men such as Bahuguna who were persuaded by the women's arguments, who provided the foundation of the Chipko movement. It began in 1972–3 in the Chamoli district of northwest India, when local people successfully organized in order to protest against the sale by auction of 300 ash trees to a sports goods manufacturer. By contrast, the local cooperative, which wanted to make agricultural implements, was forbidden by the government to cut even a small number of trees. The movement spread to other districts, such as Karnataka, and soon there was widespread resistance to the felling of forest trees that had been sold to commercial companies. Chipko means 'hugging': the name invoked a method first employed by the Bishnoi community in Rajasthan 300 years before. The Bishnoi, led by Amrita Devi, resisted the felling of their sacred *khejri* trees by embracing them, and gave up their lives in the struggle. In fact, there have been very few modern instances where villagers have literally hugged the trees to prevent the axe-men from cutting them down. The name of the movement, however, always works to

16. Chipko tree-huggers, Northern India, 1997.

suggest that in the last instance its activists may resort to hugging, as they have on occasion threatened. The idea of hugging trees also represents powerfully at a symbolic level the relationship of the people to the trees amongst which they live. In the face of increased landslides and flooding, activists in the Chipko movement pushed the campaign to a more radical level inspired by Mira Behn's early work. They agitated for a complete ban on the commercial exploitation of the forests in Uttar Pradesh, and subsequently agitated against central government development projects initiated with little understanding of local needs and the local environment.

These campaigns were formed and carried out by local grassroots organizations; individuals such as Hima Devi and Sunderlal Bahuguna moved from village to village, spreading the word and advising on methods. Although some people moved into leadership roles, as in most grassroots movements they did not achieve a public prominence comparable to the party leaders of conventional political organizations. The Chipko movement was the product of collectives of activists. Together they achieved widespread and remarkable successes in preventing deforestation in their own areas throughout the Garhwal Himalayas. From then on, the Chipko movement moved deliberately towards the conservation of the forest as an ecosystem as well as a social system. Gradually, the focus on the preservation of forestation developed into a wider political philosophy of a sustainable ecology that formed a central part of local community values.

That political philosophy could be said to be fundamentally Gandhian, though a Gandhianism that is oriented towards material, practical, and social needs, and which pushes Gandhi's ideas further in response to contemporary conditions. As defined by Sarala Behn, at a broader level it involves the pursuit of justice, of moral principles that are higher than those utilized by governments, of non-violent methods in relation to the environment as well as the community, of self-sufficiency and the empowerment of local knowledges: a resistance to centralization, corruption, exploitation, deprivation, hunger. An end to the split between private ethics of the family, and the public ethos of the values of the market place.

The Chipko movement believes that forestation programmes run by central or state government bureaucrats based on the criteria of forest science destroy both the diversity of the forest ecoculture and the resource of commons and forest as a provider of food, fuel, building materials, medicines, and so on for local people. A typical example of how this works would be the disregard of local species of trees and the widespread planting of a single non-indigenous species, such as eucalyptus, which produces no humus and therefore fails to conserve water in the soil, destroying the food system supporting plant, animal, and human life. Colonization of common land through privatization, and colonization through the introduction of exotic tree species, work in the same direction against the interests of local people, making their lives literally unsustainable by taking away their means of livelihood. Finally, such schemes are usually administered through local bureaucratic organizations, which propel the local peasantry into the clutches of a corrupt alliance of the forces of power, privilege, and property.

Since the 1970s, the struggles of women, local villagers, and tribals in Chamoli, Karnataka, Jharkhand, and elsewhere have successfully arrested many of these practices and projects, as well as enabling the formulation of a whole environmental political philosophy. Vandana Shiva and other ecofeminists have pushed these fundamental principles further towards a critique of the practices of what they call 'maldevelopment', the industrial-development model which they characterize as a neo-colonial (that is, continuing colonialism after 'independence') imposition. Such 'development' is typically organized at a state level, with international funding from the World Bank, and carried out according to the latest western ideas of what crops (genetically modified) or trees should be grown, what (chemical) fertilizers used. Market-oriented ideas of how local land should be redistributed focus on the few who are able to take on substantial debt for land purchase, while the common land on which the poorest depend for food and fuel is privatized. The many attested failures of these projects, either directly or in terms of the production of unanticipated destructive side effects, has led even development economists to begin to take seriously the local knowledges so long rejected as primitive and lacking the status of real, 'scientific' knowledge. This unauthorized knowledge empowers a politics of resistance: resisting the centralized control of the postcolonial state, resisting ideological colonization of the ethics and practices of the market place, and, most literally, resisting the colonization of local land by exotic, unsuitable plant species.

These kinds of political struggles by peasant movements have gone on in many places in India and elsewhere, and it is striking that it is women who have often been at the forefront of them. It is in India that they have been developed most fully from what has been described as a feminist sustainable development framework. Single examples such as the Chipko movement cannot be generalized to the level of a universal model: the conditions of hill and forest dwellers in India are clearly specific to a particular society, and the women of these communities cannot be the basis for a unitary category of woman, third world or otherwise. Nevertheless, given that it is rural women supporting families who are most directly affected by any degradation of their environment, the gendered force of these struggles remains prominent. Different threats can often be countered with similar methods of activism. For example, the Narmada Bachao Andolan's (NBA) extraordinarily brave and persistent populist campaign against the Sardar Sarovar Dam, part of the vast Narmada Valley Development Project, which has brought much publicized support from the writer-activist Arundhati Roy, clearly operates according to similar principles. Here, a vast infrastructural project, costing billions of rupees, is displacing 200,000 Adivasi villagers and nomadic forest dwellers at enormous human and environmental cost. The disregard for the people affected is callous in the extreme. After a long campaign, the NBA succeeded in getting the World Bank, which was funding the project, to withdraw on the grounds of its adverse human and

17. 'Damn You Dam Makers'. Local women protest against the construction of the Narmada Dam, Maheshwar, India, 1999.

environmental impact. The state of Gujarat then announced that it would contribute the lost funds. After a ruling in the Supreme Court in October 2000 that dismissed the NBA's attempt to block it through legal challenge, the project resumed its desultory, demented, destructive course. The struggle continues.

Other comparable examples would include movements of resistance to the destruction of the Amazon rainforest, or the Greenbelt Movement in Kenya started by Wangari Maathai in 1977 after she had listened to local women expressing their concerns at the degradation of their environment. Their complaints involved issues all too common for peasant peoples across the world: whereas they had formerly been able to collect firewood locally, they now had to travel for miles to find it; their seeds no longer produced adequate crops with the result that their children suffered from malnutrition; their sources of clean water had dried up. Wangari Maathai began a campaign of planting seedlings to grow trees that would provide firewood, shade, humus for crops, and prevent soil erosion. By 2000, over 15 million trees had been planted. At the same time, she led opposition to the destruction of the forest for construction development and the planting of non-sustaining export crops. The Greenbelt Movement has now spread to other African countries and around the world.

Ecology movements of these kinds tend inevitably to emerge from contexts that mean that certain elements are emphasized at the expense of others, for example, in the case of the Chipko movement, the role of inequalities of class and caste. It is here that comparable projects can usefully be brought together in relation to the priorities of a postcolonial politics. Conditions and needs will be very different for forest dwellers in northern India than for immigrant slum dwellers in East London; nevertheless, their campaigns are motivated by a similar demand for the rights and needs of all subaltern peoples (not just those industrial workers classified as the working class), a transformational politics dedicated to the ending of inequality and injustice, together with the recognition of the principle of cultural, social, and ecological diversity. These campaigns are typically organized at grassroots level rather than through a national party or international organization, though some make the transition from one to the other. The growing links between such movements increase the political effectiveness of each: despite the general distrust of technology, it remains the case that the Internet is now allowing grassroots organizations to plan and campaign much more effectively. It also offers a means of linking up and remaining in daily contact with international agencies, charities, and organizations such as Survival, Greenpeace, Oxfam, Human Rights Watch, and Amnesty. These can provide financial aid, legal advice for action in local and international courts, outside monitoring of repression, or worldwide publicity at strategic moments. Globalization operates from below in a way that contests the forces of domination and globalization from above with increasing effect.

What makes postcolonial feminism 'postcolonial'?

Can postcolonial feminism be distinguished from such categories as 'third-world feminism' or 'women in third-world politics'? At its most general, postcolonial feminism involves any challenge to dominant patriarchal ideologies by women of the third world. Such political activism may consist of contesting local power structures, or it may be a question of challenging racist or Eurocentric views of men and women (including feminists) in the first world. In the postcolonial state, postcolonial feminism begins from the perception that its politics are framed by the active legacies of colonialism, by the institutional infrastructures that were handed over by the colonial powers to elite groups, or appropriated by later elites. All women working for equality against the many obstacles embedded in such a framework engage with these kind of realities in the postcolony. Women's struggles make clearest the fact that while the anti-colonial campaigns were directed against the colonial regime towards the political goal of sovereignty, postcolonial struggles are directed against the postcolonial state as well as against the western interests that enforce its neo-colonial status. In much academic writing about postcolonialism, more emphasis has been placed on historical analysis of the processes of combating colonialism than on the political philosophy of the movements that challenge contemporary forms of power in the postcolonial state. With feminists, it has all been the other way around.

The general use of the term 'postcolonial' to mean, literally, in an historical sense, post-colonial may be applied to a whole range of different politics. Any political act in a postcolonial state may by definition technically be able to claim the term postcolonial, but this does not mean that such acts involve the politics of the postcolonial, any more than mass political movements in which many women are involved necessarily incorporate gender perspectives. Even those women whose activities can properly be described as postcolonial from a situational and ideological point of view cannot be characterized as operating according to the same paradigm. Take

> How, then, can one learn from and speak to the millions of illiterate rural and urban Indian women who live 'in the pores of' capitalism, inaccessible to the capitalist dynamics that allow us our shared channels of communication, the definition of common enemies? The pioneering books that bring First World feminists news from the Third World are written by privileged informants and can only be deciphered by a trained readership . . .
>
> This is not the tired nationalist claim that only a native can know the scene. The point that I am trying to make is that, in order to learn enough about Third World women and to develop a different readership, the immense heterogeneity of the field must be appreciated, and the First World woman must learn to stop feeling privileged *as a woman.*
>
> Gayatri Chakravorty Spivak, *In Other Worlds* (1987)

the difference, for example, between the work of two prominent Tunisian lawyers, Radia Nasraoui and Gisèle Halimi. Nasraoui remains in Tunisia to fight the human rights abuses of the postcolonial Tunisian state, without any specific feminist agenda. Halimi moved from Tunisia to France but has a history of contesting the colonial and postcolonial French state on anti-colonial and women's issues. The work of both women can be described as postcolonial, but as women activists their politics remain distinct.

11 February 1998. An ordinary morning in Tunis. A photographer takes a photograph of the lawyer Radia Nasraoui, standing in her empty office where her office equipment, her files, her computer used to be. It is not moving day. Overnight, the Tunisian security forces have raided the office and removed all her files, her legal papers, her books, and her computer.

Four years earlier, her husband Hamma Hammami, who had been in hiding and tried *in absentia* on a charge of belonging to the Communist Party of Tunisian Workers (PCOT), was arrested in Sousse, tortured by the police, and subsequently sent to the *Bagne* of Naador, a penitentiary. Twenty one months later, after Amnesty International had adopted his case, he was released. February 1998 brought strikes and student demonstrations at the universities. Several students and the usual suspects, including Hammami together with his nine-year-old daughter, were briefly arrested. Hammami went into hiding again, and was duly given another prison sentence *in absentia*. After sustained harassment of his immediate and extended family, he came out of hiding on 15 January 2002, and his prison sentence was confirmed.

Radia Nasraoui struggles against the injustices of a corrupt postcolonial state, in which arbitrary and unjust imprisonment and harassment are meted out to political opponents of the regime. As a lawyer, Nasraoui defends the rights of those imprisoned, above all those of her husband Hamma Hammami, one of the founders of the PCOT, an unauthorized political party, and managing editor of the banned newspaper *El Badil*. On 26 June 2002, World Day against Torture, Nasraoui announced that she was beginning a hunger strike. The object of the hunger strike was to demand the immediate release of her husband, to protest against the physical and moral torture to which he had been subjected since President Zine al-Abidine Ben Ali came to power, as well as to protest against 'the constant mental torture' suffered by her daughters through police harassment. The hunger strike, which lasted 38 days, gained wide publicity outside Tunisia, creating greater awareness in the Francophone world both of her husband's case and of human rights abuses in Tunisia generally. Doubtless as a result of this pressure, on 4 September Hamma Hammami was conditionally freed by the Tunisian authorities. Radia Nasraoui's courageous work can certainly be described as postcolonial in its fundamental engagement with the injustices of the Tunisian state, which she continues to fight, and refuses to leave. In this situation, she focuses on the main form of abuse being perpetrated by the state, choosing, as Mao Zedong would put it, to fight at the level of the principal contradiction of state oppression and human rights. Such an agenda is by no means incompatible with postcolonial politics, but it does not in itself emerge from a postcolonial feminist perspective in the way that the Egyptian feminist Nawal el Sa'adawi writes of her prison experiences. The same might be said of Aung San Suu Kyi's fight for democracy and human rights in Myanmar (Burma), although her attempt to establish western liberal ideology in a country organized according to very different cultural and moral principles is certainly conducted according to the Gandhian principles of moral force combined with legal challenge.

Gisèle Halimi, though born in Tunisia, was educated and qualified as a lawyer in 1956 in France. She immediately began to act as a lawyer for the Algerian *Front de Libération Nationale* (FLN) and came to prominence with respect to her legal campaign on behalf of Djamila Boupacha, a young Algerian girl tortured by the police in French Algeria in 1961. Since this *cause célèbre*, which brought her the friendship of Simone de Beauvoir and of Sartre, Halimi has defended Basque terrorists in court, and also worked as a lawyer on issues relating to women, particularly the Bobigny abortion trial of 1972. In 1971 she founded the group *Choisir*, which was formed to defend women who deliberately made public the fact that they had had illegal abortions. *Choisir*'s ensuing campaign was a major factor in the decision by the French government to make abortion legal in France in 1974. Halimi went on to become a deputy in the French National Assembly and a French delegate to UNESCO. She returned to wider public prominence in October 2000 as one of the signatories of the manifesto demanding that the French people admit and face up to the history of the systematic use of torture by the French authorities against the Algerian people, and calling for the condemnation of such practices in a public statement by the president and prime minister. Halimi has been one of the major instigators of the memory work of forcing France to confront the postcolonial legacies of its colonial history. This has initiated a profound rethinking, reworking, and re-estimation of the ethics of the ruthless French campaign to suppress Algerian independence, the effects of which continue to reverberate in both countries.

The specific conditions, therefore, for women in postcolonial states, or the postcolonial conditions in metropolitan states for migrants, vary according to location, with the result that there cannot be a single form of postcolonial politics. What makes a politics postcolonial is a broader shared political philosophy that guides its ethics and its practical aims. Postcolonialism as a political philosophy means first and foremost the right to autonomous self-government of those who still find themselves in a situation of being controlled politically and administratively by a foreign power. With sovereignty achieved, postcolonialism seeks to change the basis of the state itself, actively transforming the restrictive, centralizing hegemony of the cultural nationalism that may have been required for the struggle against colonialism. It stands for empowering the poor, the dispossessed, and the disadvantaged, for tolerance of difference and diversity, for the establishment of minorities' rights, women's rights, and cultural rights within a broad framework of democratic egalitarianism that refuses to impose alienating western ways of thinking on tricontinental societies. It resists all forms of exploitation (environmental as well as human) and all oppressive conditions that have been developed solely for the interests of corporate capitalism. It challenges corporate capitalism's commodification of social relations and the doctrine of individualism that functions as the means through which this is achieved. It resists all exploitation that results from comparative poverty or powerlessness – from the appropriation of natural resources, to unjust prices for commodities and crops, to the international sex trade. Postcolonialism stands for the right to basic amenities – security, sanitation, health care, food, and education – for all peoples of the earth, young, adult, and aged; women and men. It champions the cause not only of industrial workers but also those underclasses, those groups marginalized according to gender or ethnicity, that have not hitherto been considered to qualify for radical class politics. While encouraging personal authenticity of sincerity and altruism, it questions attempts to return to national or cultural 'authenticity', which it regards as largely constructed for dubious political purposes. It considers the most productive forms of thought those that interact freely across disciplines and cultures in constructive dialogues that undo the hierarchies of power.

Postcolonialism, with its fundamental sympathies for the subaltern, for the peasantry, for the poor, for outcasts of all kinds, eschews the high culture of the elite and espouses subaltern cultures and knowledges which have historically been considered to be of little value but which it regards as rich repositories of culture and counter-knowledge. The sympathies and interests of postcolonialism are thus focused on those at the margins of society, those whose cultural identity has been dislocated or left uncertain by the forces of global capitalism – refugees, migrants who have moved from the countryside to the impoverished edges of the city, migrants who struggle in the first world for a better life while working at the lowest levels of those societies. At all times, postcolonialism stands for a transformational politics, for a politics dedicated to the removal of inequality – from the different degrees of wealth of the different states in the world system, to the class, ethnic, and other social hierarchies within individual states, to the gendered hierarchies that operate at every level of social and cultural relations. Postcolonialism combines and draws on elements from radical socialism, feminism, and environmentalism. Its difference from any of these as generally defined is that it begins from a fundamentally tricontinental, third-world, subaltern perspective and its priorities always remain there. For people in the west, postcolonialism amounts to nothing less than a world turned upside-down. It looks at and experiences the world from below rather than from above. Its eyes, ears, and mouth are those of the Ethiopian woman farmer, not the diplomat or the CEO.

The framework of postcolonial politics is such that gender constitutes one of its enabling conditions. The inseparable centrality of gender politics to postcolonialism can be simply illustrated by contrasting it to the phrase 'women in third-world politics', the title of a chapter in a well-known textbook on comparative third-world politics. The masculist assumption there is that there is a ready-made constituency, third-world politics, and that women can be adequately catered for by seeing how they operate within it. Politics by implication is a fundamentally masculine activity and social space: the chapter will look at how women operate within a world that is not of their making. A postcolonial perspective, on the other hand, starts from the premise that there is no third-world politics without women, and that women have broadly defined much of what constitutes the political. Women therefore not only operate as political activists, but also have typically constituted the political arena in which they work.

Whereas traditional Marxist analyses had always emphasized the role of women factory workers, western feminists argued from the 1960s onwards for the political significance of women's domestic work, and of the domestic sphere in general. This was then subsumed by greater emphasis on subjectivity and sexuality, with recourse to psychoanalysis and issues of identity. Postcolonial feminism is certainly concerned to analyse the nervous conditions of being a woman in a postcolonial environment, whether in the social oppression of the postcolony or the metropolis. Its concern is not in the first place with individual problems but with those that affect whole communities. For this reason, it places greater emphasis on social and political campaigns for material, cultural, and legal rights; equal treatment in the law, education, and the workplace; the environment; and the differences between the values that feminists outside the west may encounter and those that they may wish to stand by. As activism, it involves grassroots campaigns rather than party politics. This correlates with today's decline in interest in political parties and party organizations at a national level. Not that a postcolonial politics eschews political intervention in the traditional space of the political, though it does not necessarily stop at a national level, as such political spaces customarily do.

Postcolonial politics is fundamentally, in conception and practice, a transnational politics. The new Tricontinental of the postcolonial works not through cooperation of state organizations at a government level, but operates from below across the continents through alliances of ordinary people working together.

Postcolonial feminism has never operated as a separate entity from postcolonialism; rather it has directly inspired the forms and the force of postcolonial politics. Where its feminist focus is foregrounded, it comprises non-western feminisms which negotiate the political demands of nationalism, socialist-feminism, liberalism, and ecofeminism, alongside the social challenge of everyday patriarchy, typically supported by its institutional and legal discrimination: of domestic violence, sexual abuse, rape, honour killings, dowry deaths, female foeticide, child abuse. Feminism in a postcolonial frame begins with the situation of the ordinary woman in a particular place, while also thinking her situation through in relation to broader issues to give her the more powerful basis of collectivity. It will highlight the degree to which women are still working against a colonial legacy that was itself powerfully patriarchal – institutional, economic, political, and ideological.

Typically, writing about tricontinental women's political activism profiles movements and organizations rather than parties or individuals, or analyses the oppression of particular groups, for example migrant women workers, sweatshop workers, or sex workers. This is common to writing about other subaltern forms of resistance, peasant movements, or anti-capitalist organizations. In a comparable way, only rarely do subaltern postcolonials espousing active forms of postcolonial politics achieve access to mainstream forms of political power, as did the Brazilian Luiz Inácio da Silva (Lula) of the Workers' Party when he was elected president of Brazil in August 2002. Who knows, perhaps one day Subcommandante Marcos, or rather even Commandante Esther, will become president of Mexico.

Probably the best-known example of a subaltern woman activist who achieved political power was Phoolan Devi, the low-caste *dasyu sundari* ('beautiful bandit'), as she was called by local people in the Chambal region of India where she operated as the undisputed queen of the ravines. Devi became notorious after the massacre of 20 upper-caste *thakurs* (landowners) at Behmai in Uttar Pradesh in 1981, carried out in revenge for a *thakur*'s gang rape perpetrated on her (the worst of many abuses she had suffered). After her dramatic surrender in 1983, with which she renounced her own embittered violence and rough justice, she spent many years in jail. Eventually, however, she became an MP, announcing her desire to work for the poor, the downtrodden, the exploited, and the so-called 'most backward castes'. This indeed is what she proceeded to do, though far more media space has been taken up discussing the merits, or lapses, of the film about her early life, *Bandit Queen*, than has ever been devoted to her political work. Phoolan was a dramatic and highly visible symbol of the political assertion of subaltern women and the oppressed lower castes of India. Her very presence effected a continuing protest against the deeply entrenched, oppressive treatment of Dalits in India. Phoolan Devi was herself assassinated in July 2001. As popular hero, she became the first woman to join the symbolic iconography of champions of the poor and oppressed, alongside Che Guevara, Frantz Fanon, and Subcommandante Marcos.

The untouchables: caste

Phoolan Devi demonstrates dramatically that not every form of oppression against which the subaltern postcolonial is fighting is a postcolonial legacy, though historically they often became integrated at some point. Gandhi fought the British, but he also campaigned for women's rights and for the end of the caste system, particularly its doctrine of untouchability.

In India there are four main castes, and beneath them is a fifth group known as 'the Scheduled Caste', which in fact means that

18. Phoolan Devi, with her gang, on her way to the surrender ceremony at the village of Bhind, India, 12 February 1983 (*Yugdish Yadar*).

they have no caste. The effect of this is that they are considered literally untouchable, and are, predictably, the most oppressed and exploited group. Caste is defined at birth. A quarter of the Indian population is made up of such Dalits, as they call themselves (Dalit means 'the oppressed' or 'the broken'). They do the most menial jobs, cleaning toilets, roads, and the like, and live segregated from the rest of the population in separate areas, generally on the downhill side of the drainage ditch. They have little access to education or health care, and are forced to suffer daily the indignities of being considered unclean and polluting by the rest of the population (examples of discrimination include having to remove their shoes when they walk through the parts of the village where the higher castes live, not being allowed to sit on buses, to collect water from common wells, or enter many Hindu temples). At the same time, the upper castes exploit them economically, materially, and sexually, and subject them to constant mental and physical abuse. Women from lower castes were traditionally forbidden to cover their breasts with a blouse, so as to ensure their constant availability for predatory upper-caste men. Even today, robbery of, attacks on, or rapes of Dalits are rarely taken seriously as crimes by the police, who generally disregard them and decline to take action against the perpetrators. The status of the Dalits is an intrinsic part of Hinduism, to which the idea of caste is fundamental.

Throughout the 20th century, there were many Dalit political movements contesting the degradation to which they were born, the best known of which was led by the remarkable B. R. Ambedkar, who successfully negotiated for positive discrimination for Dalits in certain areas of Indian institutional practices. In the 1970s an organization of Dalit youth calling themselves the Dalit Panthers, on the analogy of the Black Panthers of the United States, was started in Mumbai, providing a spark for the development of other militant groups across the country. Today there is a national and international campaign for Dalit human rights. But despite all the campaigns, the situation has in many ways remained as it always was. After the Gujarat earthquake of 2000, there were widespread reports that Dalits were being discriminated against in the distribution of relief. Even emergency earthquake aid was organized so as to correlate with the human degradation of the caste system. As a result of their lowly place in Hinduism, where they are irrevocably consigned to the outside, being literally outcasts, many Dalits have converted to Christianity and Islam. Others, including some famous Dalits, such as Ambedkar and Phoolan Devi herself, have converted to Buddhism.

In Sri Lanka, however, where the dominant Sinhalese are Buddhist, there is a comparable outcast group, called the Rodiya (Rodi means 'filth'). Strangely, in this context, Rodiya women have traditionally been renowned for their extreme beauty, clearly evident in the erotic photographs taken of Rodiya women by local photographic firms and circulated on postcards for the European community from the early 20th century onwards. The Sinhala majority excluded the Rodiya from their villages and communities, obliged them to wear caste-specific clothes, and denied them access to any land or work. In a cruel gesture, the only activity that they were permitted to engage in was to beg for alms. Discrimination has been far worse than that against the Tamils, who have themselves suffered severe discrimination right up to the present. It should be noted, however, that as Hindus the Tamils in turn operate their own hierarchical caste system amongst themselves.

A postcolonial politics is equally opposed to discrimination by caste or race, wherever it may be practised. It seeks to turn difference from the basis of oppression into one of positive, intercultural social diversity.

Chapter 6
Globalization from a postcolonial perspective

Che reads *The Wretched of the Earth*

> **Self-government is our right – a thing no more to be doled out to us or withheld ... than the right to feel the sun or smell the flowers or to love our kind.**
>
> **Sir Roger Casement, Irish nationalist during his trial**
>
> **for treason, 1916**

March 1965: a Britannia aircraft coming from Algiers via Prague breaks down while on a stopover at Shannon airport in the west of Ireland, and the passengers are forced to camp out there for a couple of days. They are on their way to Cuba. One night, having run out of cigars, they go into Shannon to try to see a cowboy film, but can't find one. So instead, they drop into a pub and order some beers. In the jostle of the packed bar, a local Irishman bumps into one of the Cubans and slops his beer all over his bearded companion. It was Che Guevara.

The wet but warm Irish welcome produced a few characteristic wisecracks from Che, whose great grandfather Patrick Lynch had emigrated from Mayo in the west of Ireland in the 18th century. In time-honoured ancestral fashion, Che cheerfully just ordered another beer. Much of the time in the pub, and while they waited at Shannon, Che spent talking to one of the other Cubans, the great poet and critic Roberto Fernández Retamar, who at the time was director of the famous Cuban publishing house Casa de las Americas. Che recommended to Retamar that he have a book translated for Cuban publication that had increasingly preoccupied him on the tour of Africa from which he was just returning. The book was Frantz Fanon's *The Wretched of the Earth*.

Revolutionary Africa had infiltrated into revolutionary Latin America, except of course that if the revolutionary Africa was represented by Fanon, he had come from Latin America in the first place. You could say that there have been not one but three revolutionary Africas in the 20th century: the revolutionary Africa of the Maghreb, notably the Algerian War of Independence; then there was the revolutionary sub-Saharan Africa whose insurrectional impulses were encouraged by Fanon and directly aided by Guevara in his Congo campaign; and finally the revolutionary Africa from which Fanon came – the revolutionary, or more properly militant, African-American tradition which was historically always inextricably mixed with Caribbean interventions. The famous Che-Lumumba Club, the militant all-black collective of the Communist Party in Los Angeles in the 1960s, was one iconic manifestation of that revolutionary African-Caribbean impulse, as was the revival of a black socialism, self-consciously affiliated to tricontinental revolutionary struggle, by Stokely Carmichael, Leroi Jones, and Huey P. Newton, leader of the Black Panthers. What's so striking here is that half of the name of that militant all-black collective should have been that of a white man: Che. But as a Hispanic, after all, in the United States Che was not quite white.

Che's writings and speeches show a marked change in this period – as his focus shifts from building socialism in Cuba, to a Fanonian vision of a world split between the exploitative imperialist and the progressive socialist countries. The murder of Patrice Lumumba, the talented president of the newly liberated Congo, as a part of 'Project Wizard', a CIA 'covert action program' which took place under the condoning eye of the United Nations, together with the war being waged by the United States against the Vietnamese, gave a new sense that formal independence was only the beginning of a new era of a different kind of domination by the west. The extraordinarily powerful *Wretched of the Earth* was the inspiration of that anti-imperialist moment. The book's most difficult aspect comes with Fanon's argument for the use of violence in anti-colonial struggle. He justified this on the grounds that violence, not civilization or the rule of law, was the constitutive condition of colonialism itself. Colonial rule, he suggested, was merely an attempt to legitimate and normalize the acts of colonial violence by which the country had been occupied in the first place and by which colonial rule was subsequently maintained.

After its publication in 1961, *The Wretched of the Earth* very rapidly became the bible of decolonization, inspiring many different kinds of struggle against domination and oppression across the world. When the first English translation of *Les damnés de la terre* was published by Présence Africaine in Paris in 1963, it was called simply *The Damned*. Two years later, when it was published in London, it was renamed and given the title by which it is now known, *The Wretched of the Earth*. The following year it was published in the United States, with a new subtitle: 'a Negro Psychoanalyst's Study of the Problems of Racism & Colonialism in the World Today'. By the time the book was reissued in 1968 as an African-American mass-market paperback, the subtitle had changed. Now it was 'The Handbook for the Black Revolution that is Changing the Shape of the World'. Well, it was 1968 – and why not? Think of the reversal of agency that the book itself achieved in five years: from *The Damned* to 'The Handbook for the Black Revolution that is Changing the Shape of the World'.

Fanon himself, like many of those fighting for Republican Spain or the Taliban, was an international combatant. In many respects, his cosmopolitanism, his tendency to identify with oppression and injustice in its many forms universally rather than locally, his powerfully expressed humanism, his Maoist emphasis on the revolutionary primacy of the peasantry, align Fanon with another famous internationalist revolutionary and committed activist, another déraciné man of routes, who was almost his exact contemporary and who died similarly young: Che Guevara (their respective dates are 1925–61, 1928–67). Guevara first visited Algiers in July 1963, on the first anniversary of independence, travelling around the country for three weeks, and while he was there, he struck up an immediate rapport with the Algerian leftist FLN president Ben Bella. Cuba and Algeria had already developed close relations, but Guevara and Ben Bella were particularly close in ideological terms.

In December 1964, Guevara went to the United States and delivered his devastating denunciation of imperialism to the United Nations, to the consternation of the US government. It was during this visit that Che was invited up to Harlem by Malcolm X, like Castro before him, but felt unable to go given that the US government was already incensed by his UN speech – Che judged that to speak in Harlem would be seen as an intervention in US internal affairs. So instead he sent a message of solidarity, which Malcolm X read out, adding:

> This is from Che Guevara. I'm happy to hear your warm round of applause in return because it lets the white man know that he's not just in a position to tell us who we should applaud for and who we shouldn't applaud for. And you don't see any anti-Castro Cubans around here – we eat them up.

True to this African solidarity, after his United Nations appearance, Guevara flew to Africa and embarked on a punishing round of conferences and diplomatic missions in Africa and the Middle East similar to those on which Fanon had travelled four years before – except that Guevara also followed the footsteps of the black

124

Pan-Africanist W. E. B. Du Bois and threw in a visit to China for good measure. It was during this trip around Africa that Guevara first read and lived the realities of *The Wretched of the Earth*. On his return to Algiers in 1965, he was interviewed by Josie Fanon, Fanon's widow, for *Révolution Africaine,* speaking to her of the importance of Africa as a field of struggle against imperialism, colonialism, and neo-colonialism. There were dangers, he said, but also many positive aspects, including, as he put it in an implicit reference to Fanon, 'the hate which colonialism has left in the minds of the people'. But in homage to Fanon's humanism, Guevara also wrote his greatest essay during this trip, 'Socialism and Man in Cuba' (1965), an eloquent, emotional argument for a society based on human values, that could only begin by changing consciousness itself. For Che, what he characterized as the new man and the new woman were inexorably part of the development of a new society. Socialism, he argued, cannot be imposed from above: it must be produced as an ethical as well as material value from the people themselves.

It was after that trip that Guevara was soon to lead the Cuban battalion's expedition to Central Africa, and subsequently his final, dispiriting expedition to Bolivia. In a sense, Guevara took over as the living figurehead of armed revolution from Fanon, but both men became far more famous, as iconic, dynamic legends, after their death. *Che vive*. The two were emblematically brought together in the 1966 reprint of *Les Damnés de la terre*, which, for the first time, had a photograph on its cover. The photo is not, however, as one might expect, of Algeria, but rather shows a group of African revolutionaries, men and women, engaged in a guerrilla campaign out in the bush, a photograph suggestively reminiscent of those of Che Guevara and his African-Cuban army in the Congo at that time.

Like Che, one of Fanon's greatest qualities was his ability to inspire others. His publisher, François Maspero, describes very powerfully the basis of Fanon's contemporary appeal in performative terms that could equally apply to Che.

frantz fanon

les damnés de la terre

FRANÇOIS MASPERO

19. Cover of the 1966 reprint of Fanon's *Les Damnés de la terre*.

Fanon's book, *Towards the African Revolution* (1959), cornered those to whom it was addressed with a cruel simplicity. Once the message was heard and understood, it became necessary to *participate*, to take an active stand; remaining silent could only be interpreted as a new kind of disavowal.

Numerous were those, who, like myself, discovered in *Towards the African Revolution* the basis of their commitment and the answer to 'why we are fighting', which, hitherto, had been so cruelly lacking. We saw in Fanon's appeal only an appeal to fraternity.

A similar response is given by Fanon's first publisher and editor, Francis Jeanson, author of the remarkable book *L'Algérie, hors la loi* (1955), who in his preface to the original edition of *Black Skin, White Masks* (1952) wrote:

> The Revolt might, perhaps, never attain its end but its only chance of doing so resides in those men who are too impatient to accommodate themselves to the rhythm of History, too demanding to admit that they have nothing else to do in this world – which by chance is also theirs – but to prepare, in the resignation of their own failure, the triumph of a distant humanity.

In the name of this distant humanity, there is a strong commitment to internationalism evident in Che's work as well as in Fanon's articles for the FLN newspaper, *El Moudjahid*. This is what Fanon was trying to achieve by the universalism of *The Wretched of the Earth*, and Che himself sensed this, I think, by speaking to Josie Fanon of his plan to establish 'a continental front of struggle against imperialism and its internal allies', by allying what, in the language of the left, used to be termed the colonial and semi-colonial nations, across Africa, Asia, and Latin America. Everywhere that he spoke on his whirlwind trip around Africa, Che had emphasized Cuba's identification with African liberation struggles, and the need for unity not just in Africa, but also amongst all the world's anti-colonial and anti-imperial movements and socialist countries.

127

The intellectual background of the two men was remarkably similar, a heady mixture of Sartre, psychoanalysis, Marx, and Mao. Though Guevara was as sociable as Fanon was a difficult loner, they were both men of great physical as well as intellectual intensity. Fanon's emphasis on violence at times seems to describe nothing less than his own excessive ardour, his force, stress, fury, anger, and impatience, as well as the aggressivity of language and manner that was so distinctive a feature of his personality. Add the word 'haughty' and Fanon's description of the radical Cameroonian leader Félix Moumié (known as the Ho Chi Minh of the Cameroons) sounds like nothing other than Fanon himself:

> the most concrete, the most alive, the most impetuous man. Félix's tone was constantly high. Aggressive, violent, full of anger, in love with his country, hating cowards and maneuverers. Austere, hard, incorruptible. A bundle of revolutionary spirit packed into 60 kilos of muscle and bone.

Finally, they shared a further bond: neither Fanon nor Guevara were professional revolutionaries, nor even professional politicians – rather they were both professionals who became revolutionaries as a result of a conviction that the conditions which they treated were the product of social, rather than physical or individual, ills. Their humane tricontinental socialism came out of the realities of their own lived experience and their compassion for and sympathy with the oppressed.

In this connection it is important to recall that in fact, remarkably, both Fanon and Guevara were trained doctors, who continued to practise their healing skills whenever called on even as they simultaneously carried on their day-to-day commitments to violent revolution. This apparent paradox, an ethics of healing through revolutionary violence, remains at the heart of the lives and works of both Guevara and Fanon. They thought of this by analogy with the practices of medicine itself: to cure the open wound of colonial rule by surgical intervention rather than the earlier Gandhian strategy of a therapeutic ayurvedic medicine. The challenging ethics of their politics was best described by the Martinican poet and politician Aimé Césaire in his powerful tribute to Fanon after Fanon's death:

> If the word 'commitment' has any meaning, it was with Fanon that it acquired significance. A violent one, they said. And it is true that Fanon instituted himself as a theorist of violence, the only arm of the colonised that can be used against colonialist barbarity.

> But his violence, and this is not paradoxical, was that of the non-violent. By this I mean the violence of justice, of purity and intransigence. This must be understood about him: his revolt was ethical and his endeavour generous.

His revolt was ethical and his endeavour generous. Like Guevara's, Fanon's revolt was also one of indomitable will: 'Socialismo o muerte!'

Globalization and starvation

The postcolonial world is a place of mixture. Since McLuhan invented the concept of the global village in 1968, the cultures of the world have become increasingly interlayered, mixed, and juxtaposed. Largely a product of technology, of instantaneous media systems by means of which anything that happens in the world can instantly be seen everywhere else (were it not for the fact that, in practice, what we are allowed to see is carefully controlled), the inexorable forces of globalization have increasingly brought the world's economies into a single system, particularly after the fall of the Soviet Union and the so-called Eastern Block in the early 1990s. While multi- and transnational companies look to global markets for growth now impossible to achieve in the mature markets of the west, they simultaneously lower their cost base by outsourcing manufacturing, call centres, and so on to any country that is poor and reasonably politically stable (a dictatorial regime will do nicely). There are few societies today that have not felt the impact of their place, whatever it is, in the world economy and the international division of labour.

At one level, this means certain aspects of the world, particularly the production of commodities, are being standardized, so that everyone buys the same toothpaste or razor blades wherever they may be. This may not continue to work. McDonald's, whose name has become synonymous with McGlobalization, has come to symbolize everything against which anti-capitalists are struggling. It has been reporting falling profits for the past two years and, despite serving hamburgers to 46 million people every day in 121 countries, has recently reported a loss. Maybe people all over the world have begun to realize that, by and large, their local food is much tastier and probably healthier. In general, fatty beef is not necessarily the healthiest thing to be eating in an era of BSE and animals pumped with growth hormones. Why do people always grow taller in the United States? Think about it. The story is rather different in South America, where they inject female hormones into the beef to make it more tender.

McDonald's has now released its own 'Social Responsibility Report', which stakes its claim to an ideal of social responsibility while admitting that 'the Golden Arches may represent something different in many parts of the world'. The resistance to the spread of McDonald's was probably a watershed with respect to the history of US commercial globalization. Brand globalization of US goods worked well when people around the world associated the US itself with the prosperity and freedom of the American Dream. It is hardly a coincidence that the Mexicans, who long for the good life north of the border, drink more Coca-Cola per head than any other people on earth. If you get sent back by the border police, you can sit down and console yourself with a Coke. In Muslim countries, on the other hand, where the US has become widely associated with a violent, oppressive, and self-interested imperialism, things are rather different. While Coke itself is an ideal drink in hot countries where alcohol is forbidden and the food is spicy, thirsty Muslims now opt for 'Mecca Coke', a Muslim-produced alternative that donates its profits to Palestinian charities.

The impact of multi- or transnationals goes two ways. In recent years, it has become clear that it is easier to put pressure on such companies to end practices of exploitation or environmental degradation than it is with local maverick firms that may not be amenable to complaints from far away – take the logging or mining companies in the Amazon, for example. By contrast, companies such as Shell or Nike have eventually proved themselves susceptible to international pressure with regard to their local practices. Shell notoriously allowed its Nigerian subsidiary to continue for years in a whole range of activities that contributed to the oppression of the Ogoni people and degraded the local environment. After sustained campaigning by activists (led by the Nigerian novelist Ken Saro-Wiwa until his execution), it eventually changed its ways dramatically. This cannot be said for many of the other oil companies that operate in the Niger Delta.

'Good food – Nestlé – Good life'

Some multinationals continue to court bad publicity. Take, for example, the decision announced by Nestlé (which describes itself as 'the world's leading food company') in December 2002 to pursue an action for $6 million compensation from the Ethiopian government for a business that the previous government nationalized in 1975, but whose rights Nestlé itself only acquired in 1986 when it bought the firm's parent German company. The government of Ethiopia, the poorest nation on earth, suffering from its worst famine in 20 years with 6 million people who require emergency food aid, had offered $1.5 million. Nestlé, however, was seeking full compensation, at 1975 exchange rates. The effects of the famine have been intensified by the collapse of international coffee prices: coffee supports a quarter of the Ethiopian population. Ethiopia has the lowest income per person in the world, around

$100 a year, and more than one-tenth of its children die before their first birthday. Nestlé, the world's largest coffee producer, made an annual profit of $5.5 billion in 2001. Many Ethiopian farmers are now obliged to sell their crop for less than it costs to grow it. An average Ethiopian yearly income would buy just 50 grams of Nescafé a week from 'the world's leading food company'.

The news of Nestlé's action produced front-page headlines, coverage on radio and TV news, and such an avalanche of emailed global protest that the company quickly changed its position. On 19 December the Nestlé spokesperson had said the company had to take the Ethiopian government to court for its $6 million as a 'matter of principle'. By the very next day, the company offered to reinvest in Ethiopia all the proceeds that it received from the legal claim. As the London *Financial Times* put it bluntly,

> The Swiss company, one of the world's richest and most powerful, made the offer yesterday in a bid to reduce a damaging public outcry over its long-running compensation negotiations with one of the world's poorest countries.

Notice, though, that it took that global protest, and the realization that it was potentially losing billions of turnover from bad publicity, before Nestlé conceded there was anything odd about what it was doing. It naturally makes you wonder what else the company may do without thinking too much that we do not hear about.

Nestlé has also long been the target of a campaign by the International Baby Food Action Network (IBFAN) that claims that Nestlé and other companies are breaking the International Code of Marketing of Breastmilk Substitutes in developing countries. According to IBFAN, every 30 seconds a baby dies from unsafe bottle-feeding in the third world. Chocolate and coffee manufacturers such as Nestlé have already been particularly targeted by campaigners, charities, and environmental groups in the pursuit of the standards of fair trade, whereby the local farmers who grow crops such as coffee, tea, and chocolate are guaranteed a reasonable price for their goods so that they can live above subsistence level. One successful strategy has been the development of the international Fairtrade organization which provides an alternative outlet for local producers, and offers consumers the choice of buying products with the Fairtrade label. Fairtrade goods are typically agricultural produce such as coffee, tea, sugar, rice, and fruit, but the system is now also being extended to manufactured products.

Why Fairtrade?

International trade may seem a remote issue, but when commodity prices fall dramatically it has a catastrophic impact on the lives of millions of small-scale producers, forcing many into crippling debt and countless others to lose their land and their homes.

The Fairtrade Foundation exists to ensure a better deal for marginalized and disadvantaged third-world producers. Set up by *CAFOD*, *Christian Aid*, New Consumer, *Oxfam*, *Traidcraft*, and the *World Development Movement*, the Foundation awards a consumer label, the Fairtrade Mark, to products which meet internationally recognized standards of fair trade. The founding organizations were later joined by Britain's largest women's organization, the *Women's Institute*. Fairtrade makes a real difference to people's lives:

- It challenges the conventional model of trade, and offers a progressive alternative for a sustainable future.

- It empowers consumers to take responsibility for the role they play when they buy products from the third world
  Fairtrade Foundation website, *www.fairtrade.org.uk*

Few people outside the world of business and economics regard globalization as a particularly positive phenomenon; odium is frequently heaped on the institutions that facilitate that process, particularly the World Bank, the International Monetary Fund, and the World Trade Organization. The objection to the World Bank is that it tends to make stringent conditions that conform to its own precepts of what is economically desirable, not those of the country itself. This is exacerbated by the fact that it works with governments rather than the people. It never seems to learn. Again and again, its grand schemes are criticized because the local people affected are never involved. The World Bank's Planaforo Project in Brazil, for example, designed as a sustainable development substitute for its disastrous Polonoroeste Project of the 1980s, was not planned with the involvement of the local communities whom it affected. They were only consulted after pressure from western environmental groups. The World Trade Organization (WTO), for its part, seems to be an outfit designed to facilitate entry for western or transnational companies into other markets on the best terms, while ensuring that the favour is not reciprocated the other way around, and doing nothing to alleviate the sinking price paid for commodities to the non-western world.

Poverty and famine

On the other hand, always blaming the World Bank and the WTO makes things a bit too easy. At least some of the poverty, or at least suffering, of the people of the non-western world is also the direct result of actions by their own government. One example would be famine. In the case of Zimbabwe, the real issue was why it took President Mugabe so long to act in relation to land redistribution, and why he only did it when he had lost all other reasons for popularity in the country. The fact that it was carried out in such a way as to precipitate a famine in southern Africa cannot be excused. Even if the situation was a legacy of colonialism, that does not excuse the mismanagement of the redistribution.

For some time now, historians and economists have been considering the history of famine and the extent to which it has, historically, often been either manmade or dramatically exacerbated by governments or colonial rulers. The history of famine in India and elsewhere has been famously analysed by Amartya Sen. Sen has argued that famine is not so much caused by lack of the availability of food as by what he calls the relations of entitlement. The Bengal Famine of 1943, which took the lives of 3 million Bengalis, occurred at the very time that Bengal was producing the largest rice crop in its history. Similarly, it is now known that Ireland was actually exporting food during the Great Irish Famine of the 1840s. Modern famines are largely manmade. With regard to famine, history has a habit of repeating itself.

Contemporary famines in India also operate under different conditions from those that many assume: people starve to death in India today not because there is no food, but because they have no entitlement to the food that is there. Today, more people in India suffer chronic malnutrition than in the whole of sub-Saharan Africa, and more than half of all children in India are underweight. This occurs when in fact today India produces all the food it needs, and the government stockpile of rice and wheat comprises a quarter of the entire world food stocks. However, largely because of corruption and bureaucratic inefficiency, India's Public Distribution System, which controls these vast stores, appears to be completely powerless to help those, for example in Rajasthan and Orissa, who are starving to death. In order to get rid of its stocks, which cost half its annual food budget to maintain, India has taken to selling its rice at a loss on the international market. While its own people starve to death, Indian rice exports amount to a third of the total rice exports in the world. And why does India spend millions on a space programme when more than half its people do not have enough food?

Poverty and starvation, then, are often not the mark of an absolute lack of resources, but arise from a failure to distribute them equitably, or, in the case of India, a failure of will to distribute the food that is literally rotting in central government warehouses. It would be too simple to say that all that is needed are some army trucks, since, as Sen points out, from a longer perspective distribution is not only a transport problem but also one of purchasing power and exchange. As an emergency measure, however, it is hard not to believe that transport and an adequate infrastructure for food distribution would provide relief.

Sharing resources in an unequal world

The world is rich and the world is poor. There are 20 million refugees and 'internally displaced people' in the world today. The rest of the world's population live their lives somewhere along the long drawn-out spectrum from poverty to riches. The nation-states of the world make up a vast institution of inequality, of unequal access to resources and commodities. It has been calculated that if all the countries in the world were to consume resources in the same way as the United States, at least two more planets would be needed.

You can analyse the class-income differences within countries, or you can look at the differences between one country and another. The GNI (average annual income) figures make up a lengthy hierarchical table. At the top is Luxemburg, where the income is $44,340 per person. At the bottom of this table is Ethiopia, with $100 per person. Or you can just simplify it into two categories: the rich ('high-income') countries, with a combined population of 900 million, have an average annual income of $26,000 per person; in the poor countries ('the developing world'), 5.1 billion people live on an average annual income of $3,500 per person. Half of these people live in the poorest countries on an average annual income of $1,900 per person.

These are the differences that generate global action against the economic system in which we all live. Even global action against the practices of capitalism, however, turns out not to be so straightforward. The dialectical nature of capitalism has been shown to be even starker than anyone had imagined with the recent revelation that many anti-capitalist organizations – such as Global Exchange, which seeks to close the World Bank and the World Trade Organization, and the Ruckus Society, which organized the demonstrators who shut down the WTO meeting in Seattle in 1999 – have been funded by Unilever, through Ben and Jerry's Ice Cream, the EC, and even the British National Lottery. Why is capitalism funding the anti-capitalist movements that seek to destroy it? Why did the US fund Usama Bin Laden's al-Qaeda which devastated New York, effectively creating the very spectre with which it is now at war? These are the difficult questions that a radical postcolonial politics has to confront. The danger comes from the way in which there seems to be a new kind of self-deconstructive politics at work, designed to sustain the new world order by staging its own forms of dissent. Capitalism has apparently even managed to commodify resistance to itself to the extent that it also organizes and increases the production of that resistance.

Or it may rather mean that capitalism is as divided as always, and that there are openings available for strategic interventions in the name of our future.

Chapter 7
Translation

Translating – between cultures

> as the image wears away
> there is a wind in the heart
> the translated men
> disappear into what they have translated
>   Robin Blaser, 'Image-Nation 5 (erasure)'

The strategy of this book has been to introduce postcolonialism without resorting to the abstractions of postcolonial theory. At this point, however, I want to try introducing a concept that helps to bring together some of the diverse issues and situations that we have encountered and make sense of the layered oppositional politics of the postcolonial: translation. Translation, of course, is not something abstract – it always involves a practice.

Nothing comes closer to the central activity and political dynamic of postcolonialism than the concept of translation. It may seem that the apparently neutral, technical activity of translating a text from one language into another operates in a realm very distinct from the highly charged political landscapes of the postcolonial world. Even at a technical level, however, the links can be significant. Literally, according to its Latin etymology, translation means to carry or to bear across. Its literal meaning is thus identical with that of metaphor, which, according to its Greek etymology, means to carry or to bear across. A colony begins as a translation, a copy of the original located elsewhere on the map. New England. New Spain. New Amsterdam. New York. Colonial clone. A far-away reproduction that will, inevitably, always turn out differently.

Translation is also a kind of metaphorical displacement of a text from one language to another. If metaphor involves a version of translation, it is because, as the Ancient Greek philosopher Aristotle pointed out, a metaphor is using a literal meaning in a figurative sense, so that it is no longer empirically true: 'Darling. You're an angel!' To create a metaphor is to engineer a creative lie, by saying, as Aristotle put it, what an object is by saying what it is not. Even truth, the 19th-century German philosopher Nietzsche suggested, is just a metaphor that we have forgotten is a metaphor. We could say that postcolonial analysis is centrally concerned with these kinds of linguistic, cultural, and geographical transfer, transformations of positive and negative kinds: changing things into things which they are not. Or showing that they were never that way in the first place.

In the case of translation, this change is also literally true: to translate a text from one language to another is to transform its material identity. With colonialism, the transformation of an indigenous culture into the subordinated culture of a colonial regime, or the superimposition of the colonial apparatus into which all aspects of the original culture have to be reconstructed, operate

> Because it is a systematic negation of the other person and a furious determination to deny the other person all attributes of humanity, colonialism forces the people it dominates to ask themselves the question constantly: 'In reality, who am I?'
>
> **Frantz Fanon**

as processes of translational dematerialization. At the same time, though, certain aspects of the indigenous culture may remain untranslatable.

As a practice, translation begins as a matter of intercultural communication, but it also always involves questions of power relations, and of forms of domination. It cannot therefore avoid political issues, or questions about its own links to current forms of power. No act of translation takes place in an entirely neutral space of absolute equality. Someone is translating something or someone. Someone or something is being translated, transformed from a subject to an object, like the Arab woman in the photograph in Figure 12. The Spaniard who goes to North America finds herself translated from a first-world individual to a third-world 'Latino'. The Ghanaian princess goes to the United States and finds that she has become a second-class citizen, treated as if she were just another African-American. The colonized person is also in the condition of being a translated man or woman.

Languages, like classes and nations, exist in a hierarchy: as does translation itself, traditionally thought of in terms of an original and an inferior copy. Under colonialism, the colonial copy becomes more powerful than the indigenous original that is devalued. It will even be claimed that the copy corrects deficiencies in the native version. The colonial language becomes culturally more powerful, devaluing the native language as it is brought into its domain, domesticated, and accommodated. The initial act in colonization was to translate significant indigenous written and oral texts into the colonizer's language. In this way, translation transformed oral cultures into the webs and snares of writing, into what the Latin American critic Angel Rama calls 'the lettered city', a proliferation of writing which, unlike the social construction of oral cultures, would be accessible only to a privileged few. Translation becomes part of the process of domination, of achieving control, a violence carried out on the language, culture, and people being translated. The close links between colonization and translation begin not with acts of exchange, but of violence and appropriation, of 'deterritorialization'. As the Irish dramatist Brian Friel has shown in his play *Translations* (1981), the act of naming and renaming geographical features in a landscape also constituted an act of power and appropriation, often desacralizing, as in Ireland or in Australia, where mapping became the necessary adjunct of imperialism.

However, it would be a mistake to assume that even colonial translation was always a one-way process. Travellers and conquerors were frequently dependent on the services of translators, and relied on them for understanding almost everything about the native peoples whom they encountered. The literal meaning of a large number of places still extant on today's maps is something like 'I don't know what the name of this place is' – which is the name it bore ever after. False translation has, for the most part, been considered under the framework of Orientalism, where it involves a representation of another culture without reference to the original, as, for example, in stereotyping, where the writer or artist even sometimes goes to the length of creating the image of what the colonizer expected to find – such as the fantasy of the colonial harem. False translation can also suggest the possibility of diplomacy and duplicity, what might be termed 'duplomacy', what the postcolonial theorist Homi K. Bhabha calls the 'sly civility' of different kinds of accommodation and evasion, often carried out as subtle everyday forms of resistance. This develops into a culture of lying, of the 'lying native', who translates him- or herself into the dominant culture by means of a mimicry that undoes the original.

If translation involves the power structure of acts of appropriation, it can also invoke power through acts of resistance. In a sense, this comes closer to traditional ideas about translation. Here, the aphorism *traditore, traditore* – translator, traitor – moves out of the realm of betrayal. Where the indigenous culture is being opened up for appropriation by the conquering culture, any act of translation thus involving an act of treachery, the necessary, traditionally lamented failure of translation becomes a positive force of resistance, resisting the intruder.

There are other kinds of intruder: those who choose to migrate from the periphery to the centre. Translation becomes central to the migrant's experience in the metropolitan or postcolonial city, as she or he takes on the more active role of cultural translator. Having translated themselves, migrants then encounter there other translated men and women, other restless marginals, and translate their experiences to each other to form new languages of desire and affirmation: circuits of activism, circuits of desire. Take the revolutionary routes of Marcus Garvey, for example: from St Anne's Bay, Jamaica, to Costa Rica, Panama, Nicaragua, Guatemala, Ecuador, Venezuela, Colombia, to London, and then, in 1916, to New York City. Or think of Frantz Fanon in the 1950s, moving from Martinique to France to Algeria, to Tunis then to Accra.

The Caribbean has always been a space of translation as a two-way process, through its different languages and cultures. It even has its own term for it: creolization. As the word 'creole' implies, here translation involves displacement, the carrying over and transformation of the dominant culture into new identities that take on material elements from the culture of their new location. Both sides of the exchange get creolized, transformed, as a result. Caribbean creolization comes close to a foundational idea of postcolonialism: that the one-way process by which translation is customarily conceived can be rethought in terms of cultural interaction, and as a space of re-empowerment. How can such forms of empowering translation be activated?

Empowering Fanon

When you finally drive out from Algiers, from its long arcades, its dazzling sunlit sea and secret fragrances, you come in a little while to Boufarik. High in the air before you, on the wall of the factory of the Compagnie Française des Produits Orangina, shakes the blue and yellow logo of Orangina, the fizzy drink founded by a French settler in 1936, and now beloved of all those who find themselves anywhere enclosed in the searing, sealed volume of the heat of Europe or the Maghreb.

Ah! Orangina™!

Refreshed, you leave the lush orange groves and continue on to Blida, '*la ville des roses*', another city of flowers, and of football, dominated by the bright turquoise dome of the mosque with its four tiled minarets, and the strange inhospitable Blidean Atlas Mountains towering dark cedar blue beyond.

A couple of miles beyond the city as you turn back from the steep gorges that rise above the vast Mitidja plain, the invisible dry scents of Aleppo pines finally give way to the moist, sweet smells of vineyards and orchards. You turn a corner in the road and see in the distance, its high stone walls surrounded by huge wheat fields, the huge psychiatric hospital of Blida-Joinville. Its hundred or so buildings are laid out amongst landscaped walks, gardens, and rows of trees offering shade in the summer heat.

Inside a large, solid, stuccoed house, a young woman and her son play in the quiet of the afternoon. It is November 1953. A few hundred yards away, the new *chef de service* of the Psychiatry Department at the hospital stands with the single nurse in charge at the doorway of a ward in which he sees 69 inmates, *indigènes*, natives, all chained to their beds in straitjackets. The forceful new *chef de service* stares angrily at the scene of quiet torture. He orders the nurse to release them all. The nurse stares at him, uncomprehending. In a fury, the new chief shouts his order out more insistently. One by one, the straitjackets start to be undone, unpeeled like an orange.

The patients lie there without moving, as Frantz Fanon explains to them that there will be no more straitjackets, no more chains, no more segregation in the wards between settlers and natives, that henceforth the patients will live and work together in and as groups.

Perhaps nothing in Fanon's life so decisively represented his politics of translation as his dramatic entrance to the hospital at Blida-Joinville, translating the patients from passive, victimized objects into subjects who began to recognize that they were in charge of their own destiny. From disempowerment to empowerment, from the experience of *Black Skin, White Masks* to the revolutionary *Wretched of the Earth*.

Fanon's two best-known books are themselves about translation, or, more accurately, retranslation. In *Black Skin, White Masks*, he argues that the black man and woman have already been translated not only as colonial subjects in the regime of French imperialism, but also internally, psychologically: their desires have been changed into another form, carried across into the desire for whiteness through a kind of metempsychosis. Their very desires have been transposed, though they have never, of course, actually become white. They have black skin, with a white mask.

Fanon's project is to understand this so as to find a way to translate them back again. This begins with a refusal of translation, of black into the values of white. Like psychoanalysis, it involves a detranslation, as a result of the failure of translation. In the same way, in *Wretched of the Earth*, Fanon writes of how the native has been created as, translated by colonialism into, 'a native', and inscribed with the schizoculture of colonialism as its devalued other. He states,

> If psychiatry is the medical technique that aims to enable man no longer to be a stranger to his environment . . . I owe it to myself to affirm that the Arab, permanently an alien in his own country, lives in a state of absolute depersonalization . . . . The events in Algeria

20. Frantz Fanon.

are the logical consequence of an abortive attempt to decerebralize a people.

De-cerebralization: they have been made to see themselves as other, alienated from their own culture, language, land. In *Wretched of the Earth* the task Fanon sets himself is the gaining of self-respect through revolutionary anti-colonial violence, where violence for the colonized native is a form of self-translation, the act, the grasping of agency (for Gandhi, equally, it would be non-violence). As a doctor, Fanon was equally emphatic about the possibilities of auto-translation through a dynamic, dialogic model of education, a pedagogy of the oppressed, so that the translated became themselves, translators, activist writers. The subjects, not objects, of history. With Fanon, translation becomes a synonym for performative, activist writing, which seeks to produce direct bodily effects on the reader – of which his own writing is one of the greatest examples.

Performers, players, human beings freed from their straitjackets, mental or physical. A short time after Fanon's arrival at Blida-Joinville, one afternoon the hospital's director phones the police in panic, shouting down the phone that there has been a break-out of at least ten inmates from the hospital, and that the new *chef de service* is missing as well. A couple of hours later, the director is somewhat abashed when the hospital bus returns with Fanon, exuberant, accompanied by his victorious hospital football team.

Three years later, Fanon would resign his position, on the grounds that it was impossible to cure with psychiatry the psychic wounds that were the direct result of the continued oppression of the colonial system. He was ordered to leave Algeria within two days by the French authorities, and went on to join the FLN in its struggle against French colonial rule.

Fanon spent the rest of his short life with the FLN, working tirelessly towards the ends of political and social transformation of

Algeria. As an engaged intellectual, Fanon demonstrated how important political interventions could be achieved by developing the connections between his intellectual work, his medical practice, and his collective political activism. Postcolonialism remains irrevocably haunted and inspired by his analytical work and his impassioned example, as translator, empowerer, liberator.

Translation

References

Where sources have included material from the web, the webpage address has been cited.

Introduction

Walter Benjamin, 'Theses on the Philosophy of History', in *Illuminations*, tr. H. Zohn (London: Fontana, 1973)

Chapter 1

You find yourself a refugee
Oral communications
Médécins sans frontières, *http://www.doctorswithoutborders.org*
Guardian Unlimited Special Report, 'The Refugee Trail', *http://www.guardian.co.uk/graphics/0,9749,493873,00.html*
Sebastião Salgado, *Migrations: Humanity in Transition*, *http://www.terra.com.br/sebastiaosalgado/*
UN Refugee Agency, *http://www.unhcr.ch/cgi-bin/texis/vtx/home*
The United Nations Relief and Works Agency for Palestine Refugees in the Near East (UNRWA), *http://www.un.org/unrwa/*

Different kinds of knowledge
Aijaz Ahmad, *In Theory: Classes, Nations, Literatures* (London: Verso, 1992)

'Learning Under Shelling', *http://www.poica.org/casestudies/ayda1-9-01/*

Bloke Modisane, *Blame Me on History* (London: Thames and Hudson, 1963)

The Third World goes tricontinental
Tricontinental Bimonthly
Tricontinental Bulletin

Burning their books

Langston Hughes, *The Big Sea: An Autobiography* (London: Pluto Press, 1986)

Frantz Fanon, *Black Skin, White Masks*, tr. Charles Lam Markmann (London: Pluto, 1986)

Jean Rhys, 'The Day They Burned the Books', in *Tigers Are Better Looking* (London: André Deutsch, 1968)

Tsitsi Dangarembega, *Nervous Conditions* (London: The Women's Press, 1988)

Bookburning: *http://www.ala.org/bbooks/bookburning.html*

Burning of Jaffna University Library: Vilani Perid, World Socialist Website, 30 May 2001, *http://www.wsws.org/articles/2001/may2001/sri-m30.shtml*

Attack on Oriental Institute (Orijentalni institut) in Sarajevo, *http://www.kakarigi.net/manu/ingather.htm*

Chapter 2

African and Caribbean revolutionaries in Harlem, 1924

Official UNIA-ACL website, *http://www.unia-acl.org*

Robert A. Hill et al. (eds.), *The Marcus Garvey and Universal Negro Improvement Association Papers*, 10 vols (Berkeley: University of California Press, 1983—)

Salman Rushdie, *Imaginary Homelands: Essays and Criticism 1981–1991* (London: Granta, 1991)

'Paul Robeson was tracked by MI5. Empire Inquiry linked black US star with anti-colonial politicians', *Guardian*, 7 March 2003

Fidel Castro, A Speech in Harlem, 8 September 2000,
   http://www.earth22.com/castro.html
'Castro revisits Harlem', *www.Africana.com*

Bombing Iraq – since 1920
Oral communications
Geoff Simons, *Iraq: From Sumer to Saddam* (London: St Martins Press,
   1994)
Peter Mansfield, *A History of the Middle East* (London: Penguin, 1992)
Philip Guedalla, *Middle East 1940–1942. A Study in Air Power*
   (London: Hodder and Stoughton, 1944)
John Pilger, 'The Secret War on Iraq', *Daily Mirror*, 3 January 2003
Charles Tripp, *A History of Iraq*, 2nd edn. (Cambridge: Cambridge
   University Press, 2000)

Chapter 3

Landlessness
Movimento sem terra (MST) website, *http://www.mstbrazil.org/*
The Landless Voices web archive, *http://www.landless-voices.org/*
'Brazil: President-Elect Lula Elucidates Goals', 31 October 2002,
   http://www.worldpress.org/article_model.cfm?article_id = 886
Julio García Luis (ed.), *Cuban Revolution Reader. A Documentary
   History of 40 Key Moments of the Cuban Revolution* (Melbourne:
   Ocean Press, 2001)
Jane M. Jacobs, 'Resisting Reconciliation: The Secret Geographies of
   (Post)colonial Australia', in *Geographies of Resistance*, ed. Steve Pile
   and Michael Keith (London: Routledge, 1997), pp. 201–18

Nomads
Eric Cheyfitz, *The Poetics of Imperialism: Translation and Colonization
   from The Tempest to Tarzan* (New York: Oxford University Press,
   1991)
Gilles Deleuze and Félix Guattari, *A Thousand Plateaus: Capitalism
   and Schizophrenia*, Vol. II, tr. Brian Massumi (London: Athlone,
   1988)

Ranajit Guha, *Dominance without Hegemony: History and Power in Colonial India* (Cambridge, Mass.: Harvard University Press, 1997)

Nauru: 'Paradise lost awaits asylum seekers', *Guardian*, 11 September 2001

'Afghani refugees stage desperate hunger strike in Australia', World Socialist website, *www.wsws.org*

'Woomera detention centre: "an atmosphere of despair"', Green Left Weekly (Australia), 13 February 2002, *http://www.greenleft.org.au/back/2002/480/480p10.htm*

Humans, caught in a cave

Plato, *Republic* (various editions), *http://plato.evansville.edu/texts/jowett/republic29.htm*

Tzvetan Todorov, *On Human Diversity: Nationalism, Racism, and Exoticism in French Thought* (Cambridge, Mass.: Harvard University Press, 1993)

BBC News 2 March 2002, 'Afghan caves hit with pressure bombs', *http://news.bbc.co.uk/1/hi/world/south_asia/1850219.stm*

Frantz Fanon, *The Wretched of the Earth* [1961], trans. Constance Farrington (London: MacGibbon & Kee, 1965)

Augusto Boal, *Theater of the Oppressed*, trans. Charles A. & Maria-Odilia Leal McBride (London: Pluto Press, 1979)

Michael Ondaatje, *The English Patient* (London: Bloomsbury, 1992)

Unsettled states: nations and their borders

Benedict Anderson, *Imaginary Communities: Reflections on the Origin and Spread of Nationalism* (London: Verso, 1983)

Benedict Anderson, *The Spectre of Comparisons: Nationalism, Southeast Asia, and the World* (London: Verso, 1998)

Film:

Bowling for Columbine, dir. Michael Moore (2002)

The Foreign Exchange of Hate. IDRF and the American Funding of Hindutva (Mumbai: Sabrang Communications and Publishing, 2002)

Development Alternatives with Women for a New Era (DAWN), *http://www.duwn.org.fj/*

The wall

http://www.thevirtualwall.org

Roy Moxham, *The Great Hedge of India* (London: Constable, 2001)

'Nowhere to Turn: State Abuses of Unaccompanied Migrant Children
by Spain and Morocco', Human Rights Watch, 2000,
http://www.hrw.org/reports/2002/spain-morocco

Neal Ascherson, 'Any port in a storm for determined migrants',
Guardian, 18 May 2000

'Europe's front line', BBC Crossing Continents, 21 October 1999,
*http://news.bbc.co.uk/1/hi/programmes/crossing_continents/
europe/471682.stm*

'African Migrants Risk All on Passage to Spain', *New York Times*, 10 July
2001

Film:

Touch of Evil, dir. Orson Welles (1958)

Chapter 4

Raï and Islamic social space

Marc Schade-Poulsen, *Men and Popular Music in Algeria* (Austin:
University of Texas Press, 1999)

Banning Eyre, 'Interview with Cheikha Remitti', *Afropop Worldwide*,
http://www.afropop.org

S. Broughton et al. (eds.), *World Music: The Rough Guide* (London:
Penguin, 1994)

B. Doudi and H. Miliani, *L'aventure du raï* (Paris: Seuil, 1996)

Luis Martinez, *The Algerian Civil War 1990–1998* (London: Hurst,
2000)

The ambivalence of the veil

Edward W. Said, *Orientalism: Western Representations of the Orient*
(Harmondsworth: Penguin, 1985)

Charles Taylor, *Multiculturalism and 'The Politics of Recognition'*
(Princeton: Princeton University Press, 1994)

Sahar Sobhi Abdel-Hakim, '(Inter)ruptive Communication:
Elizabeth Cooper's Photo-writing of Egyptian Women', *Cairo*

Studies in English: Essays in Honour of Fatma Moussa (2001), 355–89

Sarah Graham-Brown, *Images of Women: The Portrayal of Women in Photography of the Middle East, 1860–1950* (London: Quartet, 1988)

Frantz Fanon, 'Algeria Unveiled', in *A Dying Colonialism*, tr. Haakon Chevalier (London: Writers and Readers Cooperative, 1980), pp. 13–45

Film:

Battle of Algiers, dir. Gillo Pontecorvo (1965)

David C. Gordon, *Women of Algeria. An Essay on Change* (Cambridge, Mass.: Harvard University Press, 1968)

Fadwa El Guindi, *Veil: Modesty, Privacy and Resistance* (Oxford: Berg, 1999)

Chapter 5

Gendering politics in India

M. K. Gandhi, *Satyagraha in South Africa*, tr. Valji Govindji Desai, revised edn. (Ahmedabad: Navajivan Publishing House, 1950)

M. K. Gandhi, *Hind Swaraj, and Other Writings*, ed. Anthony J. Parel (Cambridge: Cambridge University Press, 1997)

Kumari Jayawardena, *Feminism and Nationalism in the Third World* (London: Zed Books, 1986)

Arjun Appadurai, 'Disjuncture and Difference in the Global Cultural Economy', *Public Culture* (1990) 2, 2

Trinh T. Minh-ha, *Woman, Native, Other. Writing Postcoloniality and Feminism* (Bloomington, Indiana University Press, 1989)

Hind Wassef and Nadia Wassef (eds.), *Daughters of the Nile. Photographs of Egyptian Women's Movements, 1900–1960* (Cairo: The American University in Cairo Press, 2001)

You-me Park and Rajeswari Sunder Rajan, 'Postcolonial Feminism/ Postcolonialism and Feminism', in *A Companion to Postcolonial Studies*, ed. Sangeeta Ray and Henry Schwarz (Oxford: Blackwell, 2000), pp. 53–71

Feminism and ecology

Arundhati Roy, *The Algebra of Infinite Justice* (London: Flamingo, 2002)

Catherine Caufield, *Masters of Illusion: The World Bank and the Poverty of Nations* (London: Macmillan, 1997)

Nivedita Menon (ed.), *Gender and Politics in India* (New Delhi: Oxford University Press, 1999)

Vandana Shiva, *Staying Alive: Women, Ecology and Survival in India* (New Delhi: Kali for Women, 1988)

http://www.narmada.org

Beto Borges and Victor Menotti, 'WTO and the Destruction of the Brazilian Amazon', Information Service Latin America, *http://isla.igc.org/Features/Brazil/braz3.html*

The Greenbelt movement: *http://www.womenaid.org/press/info/development/greenbeltproject.html*

Kelly Scheufler, 'The Greenbelt Movement', *http://www.suite101.com/article.cfm/history_of_peace_movements/50662*

What makes postcolonial feminism 'postcolonial'?

Le soutien a Radia Nasraoui

http://www.acat.asso.fr/courrier/docs/tunisie_cour228.htm

Hamma Hammami – Chronology of Repression

http://members.chello.at/johannschoen/Hamma.Hammami/chronology.html

Tunisia: Release Hamma Hammami and Imprisoned Colleagues

http://www.hrw.org/press/2002/07/tunis071202.htm

Simone de Beauvoir and Gisèle Halimi, *Djamila Boupacha: The Story of the Torture of a Young Algerian Girl which Shocked Liberal French Opinion*, tr. Peter Green (London: André Deutsch, Weidenfeld, and Nicolson, 1962)

Gisèle Halimi, *Le lait de l'oranger* (Paris: Gallimard, 1988)

Gisèle Halimi, *La cause des femmes* (Paris: Gallimard, 1992)

Gisèle Halimi, *Avocate irrespectueuse* (Paris: Plon, 2002)

www.dalits.org

Phoolan Devi, *I, Phoolan Devi. The Autobiography of India's Bandit Queen* (London: Little, Brown & Co, 1996)

Sidebar: References

Human Rights Watch, *Caste Discrimination: A Global Concern*
(2001)
http://www.hrw.org/reports/2001/globalcaste/
Robert Deliége, *The Untouchables of India* (Oxford: Berg, 1999)

Chapter 6

Che reads The Wretched of the Earth

William Gálvez, *Che in Africa. Che Guevara's Congo Diary*, tr. Mary
Todd. (Melbourne: Ocean Press, 1999)

Paco Ignacio Taibo II, *Guevara, also Known as Che*, tr. Martin Roberts
(New York: St Martins, Griffin, 1997)

John Anderson, *Che Guevara. A Revolutionary Life* (New York: Bantam
Books, 1997)

Ernesto Che Guevara, *Che Guevara Reader: Writings on Guerrilla
Strategy, Politics and Revolution*, ed. David Deutschmann
(Melbourne: Ocean Press, 1997)

David Macey, *Frantz Fanon. A Life* (London: Granta, 2000)

Présence Africaine 40, 1962

Frantz Fanon, *Toward the African Revolution*, tr. Haakon Chevalier
(New York: Monthly Review Press, 1967)

Globalization and starvation

Marshall McLuhan and Quentin Fiore, *War and Peace in the Global
Village* (New York: Bantam Books, 1968)

www.mcdonalds.com

Robert J. C. Young, '"Dangerous and Wrong": Shell, Intervention, and
the Politics of Transnational Companies', *Interventions:
International Journal of Postcolonial Studies* 1: 3 (1999),
439–64

World Bank Reports and Data, *http://www.worldbank.org/*

'Nestle claims £3.7m from famine-hit Ethiopia', *Guardian*, 19
December 2002

Oxfam International, *Mugged. Poverty in your Coffee Cup* (Oxford:
Oxfam Publications, 2002)

http://www.oxfamamerica.org/campaigncoffee/art3395.html

Amartya Sen, *Poverty and Famines: An Essay on Entitlement and Deprivation* (Oxford: Clarendon Press, 1981)

Project Underground, *http://www.moles.org/index.html*

Anti-capitalist movements, *http://www.infoshop.org/octo/*

'Unilever Funding', *Financial Times*, 16 October 2001

Fatima Vianna Mello, 'Making the World Bank More Accountable: Activism in South' in NACLA Report on the Americas (May/June 1996)

http://www.hartford-hwp.com/archives/42/047.html

Fairtrade: *www.fairtrade.org.uk*

Chapter 7

Translation – between cultures

Robin Blaser, *Image-Nations 1–12 and The Stadium of the Mirror* (London: Ferry Press, 1974)

Frantz Fanon, *The Wretched of the Earth*, tr. Constance Farrington (London: MacGibbon & Kee, 1965)

Brian Friel, *Translations* (London: Faber, 1981)

Vincent L. Rafael, *Contracting Colonialism: Translation and Christian Conversion in Tagalog Society under early Spanish Rule* (Ithaca: Cornell University Press, 1988)

Paul Carter, *The Road to Botany Bay: An Essay in Spatial History* (London: Faber, 1987)

Édouard Glissant, *Poetics of Relation*, tr. Betsy Wing (Ann Arbor: University of Michigan Press, 1997)

Empowering Fanon

Peter Geismar, *Fanon* (New York: Dial Press, 1971)

Frantz Fanon, *Toward the African Revolution*, tr. Haakon Chevalier (New York: Monthly Review Press, 1967)

Frantz Fanon, *Black Skin, White Masks*, tr. Charles Lam Markmann (London: Pluto, 1986)

Frantz Fanon, *The Wretched of the Earth*, tr. Constance Farrington (London: MacGibbon & Kee, 1965)

Further reading

Much information on global social movements is available on the web, but sites change too fast to be worth reproducing at length here. The best way to follow up contemporary developments for any particular issue or campaign discussed in the text is to use a search engine such as Google (*http://www.google.com*).

Introduction

Alejo Carpentier, *Music in Cuba*, ed. Timothy Brennan, tr. Alan West-Durán (Minneapolis: University of Minnesota Press, 2001)

Stephen Foehr, *Waking up in Cuba* (London: Sanctuary Publishing, 2001)

Leela Gandhi, *Postcolonial Theory: A Critical Introduction* (Edinburgh: Edinburgh University Press, 1998)

Augustín Laó-Montes and Arlene Dávila, *Mambo Montage. The Latinization of New York* (New York: Columbia University Press, 2001)

Achille Mbembe, *On the Postcolony* (Berkeley: University of California Press, 2001)

Octavio Paz, *The Labyrinth of Solitude*, tr. Lysander Kemp et al. (New York: Grove Press, 1985)

Robert J. C. Young, *Postcolonialism: An Historical Introduction* (Oxford: Blackwell, 2001)

Film:
Buena Vista Social Club, dir. Wim Wenders (1997)
http://www.pbs.org/buenavista/

Chapter 1
You find yourself a refugee
Avtar Brah, *Cartographies of Diaspora: Contesting Identities* (London: Routledge, 1996)
Iain Chambers, *Migrancy, Culture, Identity* (London: Routledge, 1993)
Arthur C. Helton, *The Price of Indifference: Refugees and Humanitarian Action in the New Century* (Oxford: Oxford University Press, 2002)
Office of the United Nations High Commissioner for Refugees (UNHCR), *The State of the World's Refugees, 2000: Fifty Years of Humanitarian Action* (Oxford: Oxford University Press, 2000)
Mike Parnwell, *Population Movements and the Third World* (London: Routledge, 1993)
Fiction:
Bapsi Sidhwa, *Ice-Candy-Man* (London: Heinemann, 1988)
Gabriel García Márquez, *Strange Pilgrims*, tr. Edith Grossman (London: Cape, 1993)
Film:
Dirty Pretty Things, dir. Stephen Frears (2002)
In This World, dir. Michael Winterbottom (2002)

Different kinds of knowledge
Roland Barthes, *Mythologies* (London: Cape, 1972)
Dipesh Chakrabarty, *Provincializing Europe. Postcolonial Thought and Historical Difference* (Princeton: Princeton University Press, 2000)
Bernard Cohn, *Colonialism and its Forms of Knowledge: The British in India* (Princeton: Princeton University Press, 1996)
Dharampal, *The Beautiful Tree* (Delhi: Biblia Impex, 1983)
Vinay Lal, *Empire of Knowledge. Culture and Plurality in the Global Economy* (London: Pluto Press, 2002)

Jean Langford, *Fluent Bodies: Ayurvedic Remedies for Postcolonial Imbalance* (Durham: Duke University Press, 2002)

Ashis Nandy, *Time Warps: Studies in the Politics of Silent or Evasive Pasts* (London: Hurst, 2001)

Edward W. Said, *Covering Islam: How the Media and the Experts Determine How We See the Rest of the World* (New York: Vintage Books, 1997)

Gayatri Chakravorty Spivak, *A Critique of Postcolonial Reason. Toward a History of the Vanishing Present* (Cambridge, Mass.: Harvard University Press, 1999)

Shiv Visvanathan, *A Carnival for Science: Essays on Science, Technology and Development* (Delhi: Oxford University Press, 1997)

Gauri Viswanathan, *Masks of Conquest: Literary Study and British Rule in India* (London: Faber, 1990)

Fiction:

Italo Calvino, *Invisible Cities*, tr. William Weaver (London: Secker and Warburg, 1974)

Gabriel García Márquez, *One Hundred Years of Solitude*, tr. Gregory Rabassa (London: Cape, 1970)

Richard Rive, *Buckingham Palace, District Six* (London: Heinemann, 1986)

Salman Rushdie, *East, West* (London: Cape, 1994)

The Third World goes tricontinental

Amilcar Cabral, *Return to the Source. Selected Speeches by Amilcar Cabral* (New York: Monthly Review Press with Africa Information Service, 1973)

Paul Cammack, David Pool, and William Tordoff, *Third World Politics: A Comparative Introduction*, 2nd edn. (Basingstoke: Macmillan, 1993)

Arif Dirlik, *The Postcolonial Aura. Third World Criticism in the Age of Global Capitalism* (Boulder, Co.: The Westview Press, 1997)

Alan Thomas et al. (eds.), *Third World Atlas*, 2nd edn. (Milton Keynes: Open University Press, 1994)

Immanuel Wallerstein, *The Modern World System*, 3 vols (New York: Academic Press, 1974–89)

Richard Wright, *The Color Curtain: A Report on the Bandung Conference*, with a foreword by Gunnar Myrdal, introduction by Amritjit Singh (Jackson: University of Mississippi Press, 1995)

Burning their books
S. Akhtar, *Be Careful with Mohammed! The Salman Rushdie Affair* (London: Bellow, 1989)
Albert Memmi, *The Coloniser and the Colonised*, with an introduction by Jean-Paul Sartre (Boston: Beacon Press, 1967)
Fiction:
Jamaica Kincaid, *A Small Place* (New York: Farrar, Straus and Giroux, 1988)
Poetry:
Aimé Césaire, *Notebook of a Return to My Native Land*, tr. Mireille Rosello with Anne Pritchard (Newcastle upon Tyne: Bloodaxe Books, 1995)

Chapter 2
African and Caribbean revolutionaries in Harlem, 1924
Elleke Boehmer, *Empire, the National, and the Postcolonial, 1890–1920: Resistance in Interaction* (Oxford: Oxford University Press, 2002)
Michel Fabre, *From Harlem to Paris: Black American Writers in France, 1840–1980* (Urbana: University of Illinois Press, 1991)
Paul Gilroy, *The Black Atlantic: Modernity and Double Consciousness* (London: Verso, 1993)
Ulf Hannerz, *Transnational Connections: Culture, People, Places* (London: Routledge, 1996)
C. L. Innes, *A History of Black and Asian Writing in Britain, 1700–2000* (Cambridge: Cambridge University Press, 2002)
C. L. R. James, *The C. L. R. James Reader*, ed. Anne Grimshaw (Oxford: Blackwell, 1992)
Winston James, *Holding Aloft the Banner of Ethiopia. Caribbean Radicalism in Early Twentieth-Century America* (London: Verso, 1998)

Rupert Lewis, *Marcus Garvey: Anti-colonial Champion* (Trenton, N.J.: Africa World Press, 1988)

Autobiography and fiction:

W. E. B. du Bois, *Dark Princess, a Romance* (Millwood, N.Y.: Kraus-Thomson, 1974)

James Weldon Johnson, *The Autobiography of an Ex-colored Man* (London: Penguin, 1990)

George Lamming, *In the Castle of My Skin* (London: Michael Joseph, 1953)

Nella Larsen, *Passing* (New York: Knopf, 1929)

Audre Lorde, *Zami: A New Spelling of My Name* (London: Sheba, 1984)

Claude McKay, *Back to Harlem* (New York: The X Press, 2000)

Bombing Iraq – since 1920

Ranajit Guha and Gayatri Chakravorty Spivak (eds.), *Selected Subaltern Studies* (New York: Oxford University Press, 1988)

Joseph A. Massad, *Colonial Effects. The Making of National Identity in Jordan* (New York: Columbia University Press, 2001)

Scott Ritter and William Rivers Pitt, *War on Iraq* (London: Profile Books, 2002)

Fiction:

J. M. Coetzee, *Waiting for the Barbarians* (London: Secker and Warburg, 1980)

Chapter 3

Landlessness

Sue Branford and Jan Rocha, *Cutting the Wire: The Story of the Landless Movement in Brazil* (London: Latin American Bureau, 2002)

Richard Gott, *Rural Guerrillas in Latin America* (Harmondsworth: Penguin, 1973)

Sol T. Plaatje, *Native Life in South Africa, Before and Since the European War and the Boer Rebellion*, ed. Brian Willan (Harlow: Longman, 1987)

Stree Shakti Sanghatana, *'We Were Making History': Women and the Telengana Uprising* (London: Zed Books, 1989)

Mao Tse-Tung, 'Report on an Investigation of the Peasant Movement in Hunan (1927)', in *Selected Works of Mao Tse-Tung*, vol. I (Peking: Foreign Languages Press, 1965), pp. 23–59

Eric Wolf, *Peasant Wars of the Twentieth Century* (London: Faber and Faber, 1971)

Photography:

Sebastião Salgado, *Terra: Struggle of the Landless* (London: Phaidon, 1997)

Film:

Morte e vida severina, dir. Zelito Viana, written by João Cabral de Melo Neto (1977)

Nomads

Mahasveta Devi, *Dust on the Road: The Activist Writings of Mahasweta Devi*, ed. Maitreya Ghatak (Calcutta: Seagull Books, 1997)

Survival International, *Disinherited: Indians in Brazil* (London: Survival International, 2000)

Fiction:

Alejo Carpentier, *The Lost Steps*, tr. Harriet de Onís (Harmondsworth: Penguin, 1968)

Humans, caught in a cave

Anne McClintock, *Imperial Leather: Race, Gender and Sexuality in the Colonial Contest* (New York: Routledge, 1995)

Fiction:

Ngũgĩ wa Thiong'o, *Weep Not Child* (London: Heinemann, 1964)

Unsettled states: nations and their borders

Joe Cleary, *Literature, Partition and the Nation-state: Culture and Conflict in Ireland, Israel and Palestine* (Cambridge: Cambridge University Press, 2002)

Philip Gourevitch, *We Wish to Inform You that Tomorrow We Will Be Killed With Our Families: Stories From Rwanda* (New York: Farrar, Straus, and Giroux, 1998)

Ghada Karmi, *In Search of Fatima: A Palestinian Memoir* (London: Verso, 2002)

Ian Lustick, *Unsettled States, Disputed Lands: Britain and Ireland, France and Algeria, Israel and the West Bank-Gaza* (Ithaca: Cornell University Press, 1993)

Mahmood Mamdani, *Citizen and Subject: Contemporary Africa and the Legacy of Late Colonialism* (London: James Currey, 1996)

Joe Sacco, *Palestine*, with an introduction by Edward W. Said (London: Cape, 2003)

Edward W. Said, *After the Last Sky*, with photographs by Jean Mohr (London: Faber and Faber, 1986)

Fiction:

Naruddin Farah, *Maps* (London: Pan Books, 1986)

Amitav Ghosh, *The Shadow Lines* (London: Bloomsbury, 1988)

Michael Ondaatje, *Anil's Ghost* (London: Bloomsbury, 2000)

Salman Rushdie, *Midnight's Children* (London: Cape, 1981)

The wall

Néstor Garcia Canclini, *Hybrid Cultures. Strategies for Entering and Leaving Modernity*, tr. Christopher L. Chiappari and Silvia L. López (Minneapolis: University of Minnesota Press, 1995)

Jeremy Harding, *The Uninvited: Refugees at the Rich Man's Gate* (London: Profile, 2000)

Fiction:

Doris Pilkington, *Rabbit Proof Fence* (London: Miramax, 2002)

Chapter 4

Raï and Islamic social space

Homi K. Bhabha, *The Location of Culture* (London: Routledge, 1994)

Françoise Vergès, *Monsters and Revolutionaries. Colonial Family Romance and Métissage* (Durham: Duke University Press, 1999)

Autobiography and fiction:

Assia Djebar, *Algerian White*, tr. David Kelley (New York: Seven Stories Press, 2001)

Assia Djebar, *So Vast the Prison*, tr. Betsy Wing (New York: Seven Stories Press, 1999)

The ambivalence of the veil

Malek Alloula, *The Colonial Harem*, tr. Myrna and Wlad Godzich (Manchester: Manchester University Press, 1987)

Marcos, *Shadows of Tender Fury: The Letters and Communiqués of Subcomandante Marcos and the Zapatista Army of National Liberation* (New York: Monthly Review Press, 1995)

Timothy Mitchell, *Colonising Egypt* (Cairo: The American University in Cairo Press, 1988)

Gayatri Chakravorty Spivak, 'Can the Subaltern Speak? Speculations on Widow Sacrifice', *Wedge* (1985) 7/8: 120–30; revised version in *A Critique of Postcolonial Reason*, 266–311

Fiction:

Naguib Mahfouz, *Palace Walk (Cairo Trilogy 1)*, tr. William M. Hutchins and Olive E. Kenny (New York: Doubleday, 1990)

Naguib Mahfouz, *Palace of Desire (Cairo Trilogy 2)*, tr. William M. Hutchins et al. (New York: Doubleday, 1991)

Naguib Mahfouz, *Sugar Street (Cairo Trilogy 3)*, tr. William M. Hutchins and Angele Botros Samaan (New York: Doubleday, 1993)

Chapter 5

Gendering politics in India

Lila Abu-Lughod, *Remaking Women. Feminism and Identity in the Middle East* (Princeton: Princeton University Press, 1998)

Tani E. Barlow, *Formations of Colonial Modernity in East Asia* (Durham: Duke University Press, 1997)

Miranda Davies (ed.), *Third World, Second Sex: Women's Struggles and National Liberation* (London: Zed Books, 1983)

Denise Kandiyoti (ed.), *Women, Islam and the State* (Basingstoke: Macmillan, 1991)

Ashis Nandy, *Intimate Enemy: Loss and Recovery of Self Under Colonialism* (Delhi: Oxford University Press, 1983)

Gail Omvedt, *Reinventing Revolution: New Social Movements and* the *Socialist Tradition in India* (Armonk, N.Y.: M.E. Sharpe, 1993)

Sita Ranchod-Nilsson and Mary Ann Tétreault (eds.), *Women, States, and Nationalism: At Home in the Nation?* (London: Routledge, 2000)

Sangeeta Ray, *En-gendering India: Woman and Nation in Colonial and Postcolonial Narratives* (Durham: Duke University Press, 2000)

Autobiography:

Sara Suleri, *Meatless Days* (London: Collins, 1990)

Film:

Kandahar, dir. Mohsen Makhmalbaf (2001)

Feminism and ecology

Rajni Bakshi, *Bapu Kuti: Journeys in Rediscovery of Gandhi* (New Delhi: Penguin Books India, 1998)

Mary Mellor, *Feminism and Ecology* (Cambridge: Polity Press, 1997)

Rosemary Radford Ruether (ed.), *Women Healing Earth: Third World Women on Ecology, Feminism, and Religion* (London: Orbis Books, 1996)

Haripriya Rangan, *Of Myths and Movements: Rewriting Chipko into Himalayan History* (London: Verso, 2000)

Vandana Shiva, in association with J. Bandyopadhyay et al., *Ecology and the Politics of Survival: Conflicts over Natural Resources in India* (New Delhi: Sage, 1991)

Thomas Weber, *Hugging the Trees: The Story of the Chipko Movement* (New Delhi: Viking, 1988)

Fiction:

Suniti Namjoshi, *The Blue Donkey Fables* (London: Women's Press, 1988)

What makes postcolonial feminism 'postcolonial'?

Leila Ahmed, *Women and Gender in Islam: Historical Roots of a Modern Debate* (New Haven: Yale University Press, 1992)

Robin Cohen and Shirin M. Rai, *Global Social Movements* (London: The Athlone Press, 2000)

Mrinalini Sinha, Donna Guy, and Angela Woollacott, *Feminisms and Internationalisms* (Oxford: Blackwell, 1999)

Gail Omvedt, *Dalit Visions: The Anti-caste Movement and the Construction of an Indian Identity* (Hyderabad: Orient Longman, 1995)

Chandra Talpade Mohanty, Ann Russo, and Lourdes Torres (eds.), *Third World Women and the Politics of Feminism* (Bloomington: Indiana University Press, 1991)

Rajeswari Sunder Rajan, *Real and Imagined Women. Gender, Culture, Postcolonialism* (London: Routledge, 1993)

Sheila Rowbotham and Swasti Mitter (eds.), *Dignity and Daily Bread: New Forms of Economic Organising among Poor Women in the Third World and the First* (London: Routledge, 1994)

Gayatri Chakravorty Spivak, *In Other Worlds: Essays in Cultural Politics* (New York: Methuen, 1987)

Gayatri Chakravorty Spivak, *The Post-Colonial Critic: Essays, Strategies, Dialogues*, ed. Sarah Harasym (New York: Routledge, 1990)

Autobiography and fiction:

Assia Djebar, *Women of Algiers in their Apartment*, tr. Marjolijn de Jager (Charlottesville: University of Virginia Press, 1993)

Rigoberta Menchú, *I, Rigoberta Menchú: An Indian Woman in Guatemala*, ed. Elisabeth Burgos-Debray, tr. Ann Wright (London: Verso, 1984)

Vasant Moon, *Growing up Untouchable in India: A Dalit Autobiography*, tr. Gail Omvedt (Oxford: Rowman and Littlefield, 2001)

Nawal el Sa'adawi, *Memoirs from the Women's Prison* (London: The Women's Press, 1986)

Film:

Bandit Queen, dir. Shekhar Kapoor (1994)

Chapter 6

Che reads The Wretched of the Earth

Ernesto Che Guevara, *The Motorcycle Diaries: A Journey Around South America*, tr. Ann Wright (London: Verso, 1995)

Ernesto Che Guevara, *Bolivian Diary*, introduction by Fidel Castro, tr. Carlos P. Hansen and Andrew Sinclair (London: Cape, 1968)

John Pilger, *The New Rulers of the World* (London: Verso, 2002)

Fiction:

Ama Ata Aidoo, *Our Sister Killjoy: Or Reflections from a Black-eyed Squint* (Harlow: Longman, 1977)

Globalization and starvation

Stanley Aronowitz and Heather Gautney, *Implicating Empire. Globalization and Resistance in the 21st Century* (New York: Basic Books, 2003)

Michael Hardt and Antonio Negri, *Empire* (Cambridge, Mass.: Harvard University Press, 2000)

Anthony D. King (ed.), *Culture, Globalization and the World System: Contemporary Conditions for the Representation of Identity* (Basingstoke: Macmillan, 1991)

Naomi Klein, *Fences and Windows: Dispatches from the Frontlines of the Globalization Debate* (London: Flamingo, 2002)

John Madeley, *Big Business, Poor Peoples. The Impact of Transnational Corporations on the World's Poor* (London: Zed Books, 1999)

P. Sainath, *Everybody Loves a Good Drought: Stories from India's Poorest Districts* (London: Review, 1998)

Ken Saro-Wiwa, *Genocide in Nigeria. The Ogoni Tragedy* (London, Lagos, and Port Harcourt: Saros International Publishers, 1992)

Kavaljit Singh, *The Globalisation of Finance: A Citizen's Guide* (London: Zed Books, 1999)

Autobiography and fiction:

Pico Iyer, *Video Night in Kathmandu: And Other Reports from the Not-so-far East* (London: Bloomsbury, 1988)

Salman Rushdie, *Fury: A Novel* (London: Cape, 2001)

Ken Saro-Wiwa, *A Month and a Day. A Detention Diary* (London: Penguin Books, 1995)

Film:

Pather Panchali, dir. Satyajit Ray (1955)

Further reading

Chapter 7

Translation – between cultures

Susan Bassnett and Harish Trivedi, *Post-Colonial Translation: Theory and Practice* (London: Routledge, 1999)

Homi Bhabha, *The Location of Culture* (London: Routledge, 1994)

Timothy Brennan, *Salman Rushdie and the Third World: Myths of the Nation* (London: Macmillan, 1989)

Fernando Ortiz, *Cuban Counterpoint: Tobacco and Sugar*, tr. Harriet de Onís (Durham, N.C.: Duke University Press, 1995)

Fiction:

Leila Aboulela, *The Translator* (London: Polygon, 1999)

Jhumpa Lahiri, *Interpreter of Maladies: Stories* (London: Flamingo, 1999)

Empowering Fanon

Paulo Freire, *Pedagogy of the Oppressed*, tr. Myra Bergman Ramos (Harmondsworth: Penguin, 1972)

Fiction:

Keri Hulme, *The Bone People* (London: Spiral, 1985)

Tayeb Salih, *Season of Migration to the North*, tr. Denys Johnson-Davies (Oxford: Heinemann, 1969)

Index

Visit the
VERY SHORT
INTRODUCTIONS
Web site

www.oup.co.uk/vsi

➤ **Information** about all published titles

➤ News of **forthcoming books**

➤ **Extracts** from the books, including titles
  not yet published

➤ **Reviews** and views

➤ **Links** to other **web sites** and main
  OUP web page

➤ Information about **VSIs in translation**

➤ **Contact** the editors

➤ **Order** other **VSIs** on-line

Expand your collection of
VERY SHORT INTRODUCTIONS

HISTORY
A Very Short Introduction
John H. Arnold

History: A Very Short Introduction is a stimulating essay about how we understand the past. The book explores various questions provoked by our understanding of history, and examines how these questions have been answered in the past. Using examples of how historians work, the book shares the sense of excitement at discovering not only the past, but also ourselves.

'A stimulating and provocative introduction to one of collective humanity's most important quests – understanding the past and its relation to the present. A vivid mix of telling examples and clear cut analysis.'

David Lowenthal, University College London

'This is an extremely engaging book, lively, enthusiastic and highly readable, which presents some of the fundamental problems of historical writing in a lucid and accessible manner. As an invitation to the study of history it should be difficult to resist.'

Peter Burke, Emmanuel College, Cambridge

www.oup.co.uk/vsi/history

POLITICS
A Very Short Introduction
Kenneth Minogue

In this provocative but balanced essay, Kenneth Minogue discusses the development of politics from the ancient world to the twentieth century. He prompts us to consider why political systems evolve, how politics offers both power and order in our society, whether democracy is always a good thing, and what future politics may have in the twenty-first century.

'This is a fascinating book which sketches, in a very short space, one view of the nature of politics ... the reader is challenged, provoked and stimulated by Minogue's trenchant views.'

Ian Davies, *Talking Politics*

'a dazzling but unpretentious display of great scholarship and humane reflection'

Neil O'Sullivan, University of Hull

www.oup.co.uk/vsi/politics

THE EUROPEAN UNION
A Very Short Introduction
John Pinder

John Pinder writes with expert knowledge of the European Union, explaining the interplay between governments and federal elements in the institutions; consensus over the single market and the environment; and conflicts over agriculture, social policies, the Euro and frontier controls. He shows how the Union relates to its European neighbours, The United States, and the rest of the world, and outlines the choices that lie ahead. He is clear about his federalist orientation, presents the arguments fairly, and is scrupulous about the facts. This is quite simply the best short book on the subject.

> 'This short, detailed yet splendidly readable book . . . is a must for anyone seeking to understand the European Union, its origins, development, and possible future.'
>
> **Michael Palliser**

> '. . . indispensable not only for beginners but for all interested in European issues. Pithy, lucid, accessible it covers recent history, institutions, and policies, as well as future developments.'
>
> **Rt. Hon. Giles Radice, MP**

www.oup.co.uk/isbn/0-19-285375-9

SOCIOLOGY
A Very Short Introduction
Steve Bruce

Drawing on studies of social class, crime and deviance, work in bureaucracies, and changes in religious and political organizations, this Very Short Introduction explores the tension between the individual's role in society and society's role in shaping the individual, and demonstrates the value of sociology as a perspective for understanding the modern world.

> 'Steve Bruce has made an excellent job of a difficult task, one which few practising sociologists could have accomplished with such aplomb. The arguments are provocatively and intelligently presented, and the tone and the style are also laudable.'
>
> **Gordon Marshall, University of Oxford**

www.oup.co.uk/vsi/sociology